The Reality of
The Resurrection

The
Reality
of the
Resurrection

Merrill C. Tenney
Dean of the Graduate School,
Wheaton College,
Wheaton, Illinois

HARPER & ROW, PUBLISHERS
New York, Evanston, and London

CONTENTS

Preface

Ever since the apostles of Christ invaded the Roman world with the gospel, the Christian church has been endeavoring to formulate its theology in language relevant to the times. The essential truth of divine revelation remains unchanged, for God is eternally the same, but the problems and fashions of human thought vary from century to century. Each succeeding period demands some new adjustment, discarding the phraseology of the past and adopting eagerly the current formulas that seem more significant.

In this creedal flux the definition of Christianity often seems to be dependent upon the terms of the latest philosophy that it encounters. During the Middle Ages Thomas Aquinas attempted to combine Biblical truth with Aristotelian reasoning. Later Immanuel Kant's philosophy led to the theology of Schleiermacher and Harnack, and today existentialism wields a powerful influence over Barth, Brunner, and Bultmann. Is there any inherent principle or symbol by which the gospel can be defined without resorting to extraneous forms?

The author believes that the resurrection of Christ can supply the framework for Christian theology because it marks the intersection of the temporal and eternal worlds, of material existence and spiritual life. Because the event is supernatural, it expresses the essence of God's revelation; because it is historical, it is a genuine part of human experience. The resurrection is a permanent witness to the love, power, holiness, and redemptive pur-

7

pose of God and is also a fact which must be accepted as part of history. It cannot be dismissed as a speculative venture of the intellect which is possibly, but not necessarily, true.

For this reason the resurrection is perpetually relevant to the intellectual and spiritual problems of the world. The event provides a foundation for faith; its imagery contains the framework for a new life. The New Testament recognizes both of these uses, for it says, "If Christ hath not been raised, your faith is vain; ye are yet in your sins" (I Cor. 15:17), and, "If then ye were raised together with Christ, seek the things that are above, where Christ is, seated on the right hand of God" (Col. 3:1). By this one great fact all theology can be integrated. Revelation, incarnation, redemption, sanctification, and eschatology reach their fullest development in the demonstration of the divine triumph over death.

The purpose of this book is not to defend a doctrine that is no longer tenable but to show that the resurrection has a direct bearing upon contemporary intellectual and spiritual tensions. A coherent system of theology that will embrace the emergent problems of the age must also include the continuum of God's historical action in His past dealing with the world. The intent is not to debate detailed philosophical issues but to present a cogent statement of the Biblical truth and to let the reader apply it for himself.

The author is indebted to the Alumni Association of Wheaton College for a grant in the spring semester of 1959 which afforded time for beginning this book. The friendship and cooperation of the administration and faculty of Wheaton College and the interest of former students have been strong encouragement for the project.

Acknowledgments are due to Faber and Faber Ltd. of London for permission to quote from *The Easter Enigma* by Michael C. Perry; to the *Saturday Evening Post* and to Dr. Reinhold Niebuhr for permission to quote from his article "The Religious Traditions of Our Nation"; and to Westminster Press for the use of quotations from *The New Testament and Mythology*, by Burton H. Throckmorton. Scripture quotations are taken from the American Standard Version of the Revised Bible.

The author owes a special debt of gratitude to his wife, Helen J. Tenney, for wise editorial aid, and to Miss Joy Kinslow and Mrs. Carol Currie, who assisted in copying the manuscript.

MERRILL C. TENNEY

Wheaton College
Wheaton, Illinois
January, 1963

The Reality of
The Resurrection

I The Relevance
of the Resurrection

Since the edict of toleration promulgated by the Roman emperor Constantine in the fourth century, Christianity has been the dominant religion of western Europe. The decaying paganism of the empire and the ethnic superstitions of the surrounding barbarians yielded slowly until the nations became at least nominally Christian. During the age of discovery beginning with the fifteenth century, numerous explorers opened the American continents and parts of Africa and Asia to colonization and enlarged the borders of professing Christendom. In spite of fierce external opposition and internal dissension and defection, the Christian church exerted immeasurable influence upon the civilized world. The nations in which Christianity flourished became prosperous and powerful, while non-Christian nations attained a lesser degree of political freedom and economic strength.

Now a historical crisis confronts the church. Nations dormant for centuries are awaking and grasping for power. The hitherto silent millions of Japan, India, China, and Africa are shaking off illiteracy, famine, disease, and poverty, are making new alliances and demanding a hearing in the councils of the European powers. Not only are they wielding political influence which may seriously upset the balance of power formerly favoring the "Christian nations," but they are also adopting and defending philosophies devoid of any faith, chief of which is communism. A new civilization is being born which by its antecedents and nature is hostile to Christ.

The danger of this hostility is not negligible, for the rapidly increasing population of non-Christian lands is a cause for serious alarm. China, where the church is suppressed or enslaved, has a population of 669,000,000, which may reach one billion by the turn of the century. The majority of India's 400,000,000 inhabitants are devotees of pagan deities. The Arab world, solidly Moslem, is a bitter foe of the gospel, and Russia, officially committed to atheistic communism, has already declared its militant purpose of global domination. By the inexorable process of birth, Christians are rapidly losing the political and social leadership of society. Their very ethics are a disadvantage, for Christian graces curb the ruthlessness of conquest, while pagan or atheistic peoples have no restraining inhibitions.

Growing nationalism has reversed the trend of twentieth-century colonialism, and missionary activity is becoming a two-way street. From a Moslem mosque in Washington, D.C., capital of the largest "Christian" nation in the world, the call to prayer is sounded forth five times a day, summoning the faithful to their devotions. The Crescent is challenging the Cross on its own territory. Zen Buddhism is becoming a popular fad in American society. The change of religious and social trends is already so marked that the current era is being called "post-Christian," and its atmosphere is compared to the pre-Constantinian period of church history.

Against this menacing tide of resurgent paganism there is only one adequate defense. Military might is useless, for neither submarines, nor bombers, nor guided missiles are able to halt the slow infiltration of alien philosophies. No coalition of denominations can exercise sufficient political or social pressure to preserve Christian ideals and teaching if convictions crumble. Effective strategy for survival does not lie in devising new weapons for exterminating enemies but in a re-examination and reaffirmation of basic theology. Christianity dispelled the darkness of paganism in the first seven centuries of the present era and won its way in the chaos following the collapse of the Roman empire, not by lobbying or by fighting, but by the unique dynamic of its truth. As Paul said, "The weapons of our warfare are not carnal, but mighty through God to the pulling down of strong holds; casting down imaginations, and every high thing that exalteth itself against the knowledge of God, and bringing into captivity every thought to the obedience of Christ" (II Cor. 10:4-5, KJ).

The modern church suffers from an uncertainty that has almost paralyzed her ability to cope with this dilemma. Feeling her weakness because of division and schism, she has sought to remedy it by organizational union. Old rifts between Christian groups caused by differences of nationality, of polity, and of doctrine are being closed, and new unions are arising. Unity is commendable; but it cannot be achieved by arbitrarily ignoring all differences as inconsequential. The abandonment of essential doctrines may foster the kind of religious association which cultivates amiability at the expense of truth. No firm resistance to materialism and paganism can ever be offered by a Christianity which has bartered its convictions for an insipid geniality. Only a positive message, proclaimed unitedly and incisively, will make any impression on this tough-minded generation.

The formulation of a convincing message is difficult to achieve. The desire to perpetuate historic theological values may cause tensions among the adherents of evangelical Christianity. Each sect has inherited a viewpoint or an emphasis which may be Biblical in origin and amply warranted by the conditions that produced it. Reformed doctrine emphasized the sovereign grace of God to counteract the papal teaching of salvation by works; Methodist emphasis on experience stresses the necessity of personal regeneration. The individual teachings may be sound, but when they become causes of controversy rather than contributions to a balanced gospel, they may be obstacles to an effective witness. Some redefinition of creed is necessary if Christian soldiers are to be "one in hope and doctrine, one in charity."

Any reassessment of theology must begin with an affirmation of faith rather than with a denial. The question is not "How much can be abandoned for the sake of agreement?" but "What must be retained as unalterable and final?" The process of separating truth from error and the essential from the peripheral is serious business, for it affects the destiny of Christians both now and hereafter. A vague hypothesis or an unconfirmed legend is an insufficient foundation for building either a civilization or a personal hope; the doubts and conflicts of this generation cannot be resolved by abstractions.

The contrast between a vital faith and empty superstition is apparent in the New Testament. Paul, the best-known missionary of the first century, encountered widespread materialism and skepticism. The temples of false gods, in which flourished the furtive trickery of a grafting priesthood and the unblushing immorality of a depraved populace, stood in the market place of every city. Indulgence had become the highest good; futility was the predominant mood. Sex, sophistication, and success were the keynotes of the prevailing culture.

The gospel of Christ, which infused a new dynamic into that bewildered and corrupt world, was not without rivals. Mithraism proclaimed a god of virtue and light, who had overcome the power of evil by sacrifice and could confer everlasting life upon his worshipers. The mystery religions promised participation in divine secrets to their initiates. The philosophers who scorned the trivial legends of the gods offered the religion of reason— for a price—on every street corner. Christianity was not unique because it insured salvation by a sacrifice for sins, nor because it stressed personal ethics, nor even because it guaranteed immortality to believers. Its distinctive attribute was the supernatural power of the living God, manifested historically by the resurrection of Christ from the dead.

Although there have always been skeptics who have rejected the concept of resurrection, a more open attitude has recently become apparent. Physical science has gradually begun to acknowledge the existence of spiritual being. Sir James Jeans, an eminent physicist, once remarked that the universe was more like a great thought than like a machine. Psychology has realized the necessity of a new vocabulary to explain the action of the human mind. The intricacy of nervous reactions and the amazing power of the will demand the recognition of personality as a force distinct from the mechanical processes of the cosmos. Progress in physics and psychology has revealed how vast and complicated are the external world of matter and the internal world of mind. Though many riddles have been resolved by investigation, the numerous mysteries still unexplored enhance the credibility of God's creative intervention.

In the light of modern physics the resurrection of Christ seems less improbable than it did a century ago, since new properties and types of matter have been discovered. Recent psychology, in contrast to an older mechanistic behaviorism, has tended to show that the human mind may possess powers that transcend matter. The historical evidence supporting the resurrection is still valid, just as the physical phenomena of bygone generations demonstrate the latest discoveries in physical law; and the theology of the resurrection is still applicable because death and life have not ceased to be vital issues.

The gospel of Christ began with the message of the resurrection, for its foundation was an event, not a web of arguments. The creative life of God was manifested in human history, located definitely in space and time. Christ, the incarnate God, experienced the tensions and frustrations to which humanity is subject, and even endured the agonizing and humiliating death of the cross, yet He was not overcome. The bonds of death could not confine Him; in the words of Peter, "it was not possible that he should be holden of it [death]" (Acts 2:24). Because this divine act is a part of recorded experience, it is proof in understandable terms that God can transcend death by life and that He has opened a new dimension of existence to believers in Christ.

Without participating in the resurrection life of Christ, existence is progress to doom. Sin, like chain fission, produces continuing and cumulative effects. Each evil act, conscious or unconscious, brings in its wake misery and bondage. Seeking to escape from the consequence of his own deeds, man finds that he becomes involved in other evils which further complicate his fate. The inexorable law that "whatsoever a man soweth, that shall he also reap" fosters extreme pessimism. If man must inevitably reap the evil that he sows, his end will assuredly be destruction. Only the interposition of another power strong enough to arrest the downward trend can effect a permanent deliverance. The resurrection is not only the proof of divine ability to save man but the unmistakable demonstration that God has already acted. Whereas death is the penalty and result of sin, the risen Christ has made it the gateway to a new life. "If any man is in Christ, he is a new creature: the old things are passed away; behold they are become new" (II Cor. 5:17). Salvation was accomplished and a new era was introduced by Christ's resurrection.

The interpretations of historical events may differ with the knowledge or prejudices of scholars, and the importance assigned to them may change with the perspective from which they are viewed, but the events themselves are irrevocable. For example, the Yalta conference of World War II may be evaluated from varying viewpoints and with widely differing conclusions, but its historical reality and its effect upon the political fate of Europe remain undisputed. Future historians may disagree with current interpretation, but they cannot ignore the fact. Similarly, the resurrection demands the attention of those who contemplate the basic problems of death and life, for it has thrust into them a new factor which must be included in evaluating the whole of human experience. Any attempt to explain the process of history will be incomplete without it. The resurrection is permanently relevant to any scheme of thought.

The troubled world of the present century is perplexed by the paradox of its own progress. Through the application of scientific principles unlimited comforts and resources are available, yet more people live on the brink of starvation than ever before. The secrets of the universe are being unriddled one by one, yet they have become a menacing means for self-destruction. With vastly increased facilities for understanding and enjoying life, fewer people possess a sense of security and purpose, for they have no concept of the meaning of life, nor any certainty of its continuance. The resurrection is relevant to the human need for purpose and assurance. Though it occurred nineteen centuries ago, its inherent nature of continuing life and its constant applicability to recurring problems make it timeless. The event is fixed in history; the dynamic is potent for eternity.

II   *Pre-Christian Concepts*

An adequate consideration of the resurrection of Jesus Christ necessitates an understanding of its antecedents. Both in pagan lore and in Jewish Scripture the conflict of life and death has been a dominant theme. Even in prehistoric times the burial of tools and ornaments with the dead indicated hope of continued existence. The Egyptian *Book of the Dead,* the clay tablets of Phoenicia and of Babylon, and the legends of the Greeks reflect the yearning for immortality expressed more poignantly in David's agonized cry over the death of his son: "I shall go to him, but he will not return to me" (II Sam. 12:23).

The Pagan Myths

The ancients dreaded death, for it terminated joyous human activities and ushered its victim into the gloomy and mysterious realms of the underworld. Homer's description of the slaying of Hector illustrates their despair: ". . . the shadow of death came down upon him, and his soul flew forth of his limbs, and was gone to the house of Hades, wailing her fate, leaving her vigor and youth."[1]

Occasional gleams of hope appear in Greek mythology. One

---

[1] *Iliad,* XVII.

of the most dramatic tales concerns Alcestis, wife of King Admetus of Thessaly. He was doomed to death for offending the gods but was granted a reprieve by the intercession of Apollo, provided that he find someone to die in his place. Alcestis volunteered to be his substitute, and gladly surrendered herself to the wrath of the gods. Moved by pity, Hercules descended to Hades and rescued her.

A similar legend relates the story of Orpheus, the master of the lyre, whose wife Eurydice was poisoned by a snake bite. Disconsolate over her loss, Orpheus pursued her to Hades. There his music so charmed Pluto, the god of the nether world, that he agreed to release Eurydice on condition that Orpheus not look backward until they reached the surface of the earth. Approaching the gates of Hades, Orpheus stole a backward glance to assure himself that Eurydice was still following. Stretching out her arms to him in a piteous farewell, she vanished. Death remained the master of its prey.

Pluto himself, according to another myth, stole Persephone, the daughter of the goddess Demeter, and carried her to the underworld to be his queen. Because of her mother's protests, the gods intervened, and Pluto allowed her to return to earth eight months of the year on condition that she remain with him the other four months. The legend is a personification of the cycle of vegetation, which dies in the fall and reappears four months later in the spring.

Closely related to these myths were the mystery religions. One of the most popular was the Egyptian cult of Isis and Osiris. Osiris was the son of Seb, the earth god, and Nut, the sky goddess; Isis was his sister and consort. Under his tutelage men learned how to raise grain and grapes and emerged from a state of savagery into an agricultural civilization. His brother Set, the god of the underworld, conspired against him. Capturing Osiris by a trick, Set sealed him into a coffin which he cast into the Nile. The coffin floated down the river and was finally stranded on the shores of Phoenicia. Isis traced the body, which she carried back to Egypt; but Set, seizing it again, dismembered it and flung the severed parts into the Nile. Patiently Isis regathered the pieces and resuscitated the body, after which Osiris became lord of the underworld.

These grotesque tales were interpreted by analogy to mean that life can emerge unscathed from death, and the cults founded upon them promised to their worshipers a share in the immortality of the god. No elaborate theology was connected with the dramatic emotional re-enactments of the god's experience in which the initiate participated. The appeal of the cultic rites was enhanced by torchlight processions, lustrations, special vestments, sacrifices, vigils, and prayers. The accompanying element of secrecy intrigued curiosity and created the feeling of brotherhood between those who were initiated into the mysteries, and of superiority over those who were not.

Undoubtedly the legends revealed a vague longing for life beyond death, but they provided no historic basis for certainty, nor could their principal actors impart life to mortal suppliants. Wallis Budge, in commenting upon the Osiris legend, reinforces this viewpoint: ". . . the soul and the spirit of the righteous passed from the body and lived with the beatified and the gods in heaven; but the physical body did not rise again, and it was believed never to leave the tomb. There were ignorant people in Egypt who, no doubt, believed in the resurrection of the corruptible body . . . but the Egyptians who followed the teaching of his sacred writings knew that such beliefs were not consistent with the views of their priests and of educated people in general."[2]

Although the cults long preceded the rise of Christianity, they cannot be considered a source for Christian doctrine. The conflicts and caprices of the gods reflect the imagination of a primitive people; the Christian message originates from the life of a historic person. There is no record of a hero like Osiris who was dismembered and subsequently restored by supernatural intervention, but the resurrection of Christ can be located definitely in space and time. Participation in the mysteries imposed no ethical obligation upon the worshiper, but Paul said, "If then

---

[2] E. A. Wallis Budge, *Egyptian Ideas of the Future Life* (London: Kegan Paul, Trench, Trubner & Company, Ltd., 1900) , p. 167.

ye were raised together with Christ, seek the things that are above
. . ." (Col. 3:1). The differences between the current myths and
the teaching of the New Testament were greater than any re-
semblances and preclude the idea that Christian theology evolved
from a facile syncretism of pagan concepts and Jewish hopes. The
popular nonphilosophical religion of the man in the street had
little expectation of immortality and no definite idea of physical
restoration.

Greek philosophy entertained no conception of a resurrection
of the body. Socrates, whose argument for immortality has been
preserved in the *Phaedo* of Plato, discussed at length the basis
for believing in the survival of the human spirit. He argued that
the soul, which gives life to the body, cannot die, else it would
lose its inherent quality of life, and if it cannot die, it must be
immortal.[3] The body is, therefore, not the true man, for it is
subject to decay and death. Since the continuance of the soul
demonstrates immortality, the resuscitation of the body would
be unnecessary. The later Platonic philosophy developed the idea
that the body was essentially a prison from which the soul longed
to escape, in order to attain freedom from evil and from the
restrictions of physical limitations. A resumption of physical
existence would therefore be undesirable, since it would be only
a return to earthbound slavery.

Neither the philosophy of Stoicism nor that of Epicureanism
foreshadowed physical resurrection. Stoicism, being pantheistic,
considered the individual a fragment of the World-Soul. His
identity persisted only until death, or possibly to the end of time.
At death or at the final conflagration he would be reabsorbed
into the World-Soul. Death brought a welcome end to suffering,
labor, and perplexity, which for the Stoic was an accepted means
of withdrawing from the problems of life. "When the farce is
ended, ring down the curtain" was his dictum.

Epicureanism, being materialistic, taught that all existence
consisted of atoms which might temporarily be organized in a
certain form but which would change their form later to become

---

[3] *Phaedo*, 80, 81, 106.

a different substance. If the structure of the body were dissolved by death, the individual would cease to exist. The disintegration of the flesh and the absorption of its elements into other chemical combinations or organisms would therefore be an insurmountable bar to believing in a resurrection. It is small wonder that when Paul spoke at Athens of the resurrection of the dead, the Stoics and Epicureans openly ridiculed him.

These concepts of the pagan world illustrate two trends, contradictory in a sense, and yet not inconsistent. Everywhere men were groping for some reality that would enable them to face death with equanimity. Whether they attached themselves to the emotional rituals of the cults or accepted the calmer reasoning of the philosophers, they were dissatisfied with the nebulous legends of their fathers and with the despairing cries of the poets, who regarded death as the end of everything good and pleasant. For this reason, they were more favorably disposed to accept the gospel of the resurrection, though they could not have originated it. At the same time, they had no tangible evidence of life beyond the grave and, by their own hopelessness and inability to find logical reasons for immortality, they were prejudiced against the Christian viewpoint.

Paganism was not the matrix of this doctrine, nor is there in its legends any analogous concept. The teaching of the New Testament came to the Graeco-Roman world with a message which had not previously been proclaimed in the temples of the gods or in the halls of the philosophers. What was its origin?

The Hebrew Scriptures and Apocrypha

The natural source would be the Jewish Scriptures, since they were the acknowledged basis for early Christian preaching. In them the apostles had found warrant for proclaiming Jesus of Nazareth to be the Messiah (Acts 17:1-3) and had used their prophecies specifically to undergird the declaration that He must rise from the dead. If there was a continuity of revelation between the prophets of the Old Testament and the apostles of the New Testament, one might logically expect to find fore-shadowings of this truth in the sacred writings of the previous age.

The first hint of the concept of future life is found in the words of Jacob, speaking of Joseph, whom he thought to be dead: "I will go down to Sheol to my son mourning" (Gen. 37:35). Jacob cherished no hope of Joseph's returning to him, nor did he anticipate his son's resurrection since he understood the dis-embodied state to be final. The Pentateuchal law contains no clear reference to life beyond the grave either in the Decalogue or in the religious and civil ordinances that accompany it. There are occasional allusions to the unseen world of Sheol, but it is comparatively unimportant to the theology of Israel prior to the Exile.

Two miracles of restoration to life were performed by Elijah and Elisha. The similarity of the cases is obvious: one concerned the son of the widow with whom Elijah had stayed during the years of famine (I Kings 17:17-24); the other, the son of the Shunammite woman who had often been Elisha's hostess (II Kings 4:8-37); both involved young boys and only sons; in both instances the prophet was summoned by the mother; the resusci-tation of each was accomplished by the prophet's direct interven-tion. The occurrences indicate the possibility of a return from death, though they involved no change of physical nature or powers. They were isolated miracles rather than precedents for reasoning. Nevertheless they indicate that bodily restoration took place and was acknowledged under the Old Testament dispensa-tion, so that the miraculous renewal of life cannot be excluded from consideration.

In the books of poetry and prophecy there are a few veiled references. The second Psalm acknowledges the divine sonship of the Messiah. The sixteenth Psalm declared a personal confi-dence that the writer's soul would not be abandoned to the world of the dead (Sheol) nor his body to decay. Both of these were later applied to the Messianic status of Christ by the writers of the New Testament (Acts 4:25, 26; 2:25-31). The prophecies of Hosea (6:2), Isaiah (26:19, 20), and Ezekiel (37) are more general in scope and do not provide an adequate criterion for estimating the prevalence of this concept.

The prophecy of Daniel, "Many of them that sleep in the dust of the earth shall awake, some to everlasting life, and some to shame and everlasting contempt" (Dan. 12:2), is, according to Schürer, the first plain expression of resurrection in the Old Testament.[4] Coming at the beginning of the Exile, it marked a new trend of Jewish thought.

The captives of Israel residing in Babylon had been severed from their temple. Because their ritual had been interrupted and their national life disorganized, the devout followers of Jehovah were thrust back to a stronger individual faith. Community life centered in the family and synagogue rather than around a ritual and a temple. The question of individual immortality, stimulated possibly by the competition of other religions, may have evoked the divine assurance transmitted through the prophet.

Occasional references in the Apocrypha and Pseudepigrapha of the inter-testamental period enable one to follow the progress of Jewish thought between the Testaments. One of the Maccabean martyrs said to his tormentors, "It is good, being put to death by men, to look for hope from God to be raised up again by him: as for thee, thou shalt have no resurrection to life."

The mother of this martyr, who had witnessed his death, commented, "Doubtless the Creator of the world, who formed the generation of man, and found out the beginning of all things, will also of his own mercy give you breath and life again, as ye now regard not your own selves for his laws' sake" (II Macc. 7:13, 14, 23).

The same hope is expressed elsewhere: ". . . he was mindful of the resurrection, for if he had not hoped that they that were slain should have risen, it had been superfluous and vain to pray for the dead" (II Macc. 13:43, 44).

The quotations reflect a firm belief in the bodily resurrection of the individual, yet they do not predicate it specially of the

---

[4] Emil Schürer, *A History of the Jewish People in the Time of Christ,* Division II, Vol. II (New York: Charles Scribner's Sons, 1891), p. 138.

Messiah. Other apocryphal works of the same era present a different viewpoint. *The Wisdom of Solomon,* written in the first century before Christ,[5] suggested that the body is only a temporary dwelling place for the soul, which is pre-existent (viii, 20) and which survives the death of the body (xv, 8). The *Book of Jubilees,* written probably one century previously, presupposed a continued existence of the soul apart from any resurrection (II, 24).[6] This accorded with the Greek view of the immortality of the soul, rather than with the late Jewish concept.

The writer of IV Maccabees agreed with the Hellenistic concept of an eternal and blessed life of pious souls in another world rather than in a corporeal resurrection (IV Macc. 13:16; 15:2; 17:5, 18).

Immortality is denied by the author of Ecclesiasticus, who declared that ". . . all things cannot be in man, because the son of man is not immortal" (17:31). Later, however, the same writer said, "The knowledge of the commandments of the Lord is the doctrine of life; and they that do things that please him shall receive the fruit of the tree of immortality" (19:19).

In the post-exilic period, following the Restoration, Hebrew thought concerning eschatology was evidently in flux. Realizing that national existence was precarious and that the older solidarity of worship and of destiny was dissolving, the people became increasingly interested in personal salvation. The confusion of eschatological teaching is well illustrated by the disagreement between the Sadducees, or priestly party, who denied a bodily resurrection, and the Pharisees, the popular orthodox party, who defended it (Acts 23:8). The doctrine had not been clearly defined or finally settled by the rabbis and remained indefinite in the minds of the laity.

Two conclusions may be drawn from the rather scanty evidence. First, there was sufficient teaching concerning a bodily resurrection to make the Christian doctrine plausible to Jewish hearers. There is no evidence that the rank and file of the populace in Jerusalem who first listened to the apostolic declaration

---

[5] *Ibid.,* Vol. III, pp. 233, 234.

[6] *Ibid.,* p. 138.

rejected it on the grounds of inherent improbability or novelty. Second, the idea was not so essential a part of Jewish theology that it would be read into the phenomena of the life of Jesus or arbitrarily superimposed upon His teachings. His predictions of rising from the dead and His interpretation of the Old Testament were original with Him; they were not the echoes of current theology that He had absorbed and repeated unthinkingly.

Furthermore, the Old Testament nowhere specifically attributed bodily resurrection to the Messiah. The latent predictions in typology and prophecy were not sufficiently self-evident to enable Jewish theologians to create the doctrine. They were illuminated by the interpretations of Jesus, who correlated the witness of the Scriptures concerning Himself, explaining for His disciples what they had never discerned through their own reading. The resurrection of the body is, therefore, a concept fully developed only after the manifestation of Christ, who was Himself the pattern, and the exponent of its meaning.

An additional word must be said concerning the prophetic foreshadowings of the event. When they are expressed in language that implies a return from death, the primary application concerns the nation, not individuals. Hosea used the figure to prophesy revival after national repentance: "Come, and let us return unto Jehovah; for he hath torn, and he will heal us; he hath smitten, and he will bind us up. After two days will he revive us: on the third day he will raise us up, and we shall live before him" (Hos. 6:1-2). This enigmatic prediction should be interpreted in the light of his further utterance, "When Ephraim spake . . . he exalted himself in Israel: but when he offended in Baal, he died" (13:1). "Death" was symbolic of Israel's alienation from God, the source of all spiritual life; the return to God would be a restoration to life comparable to a national resurrection.

Isaiah expressed the same principle in his prophecy: "Thy dead shall live; my dead bodies shall arise. Awake and sing, ye that dwell in the dust: for thy dew is as the dew of herbs, and the earth shall cast forth the dead" (26:19). The context dealt with the sorrows and judgments of Judah, and with promise of restoration. The revivification of the nation was the model for the idea of resurrection.

Ezekiel's well-known description of the valley of dry bones provides another example (Ezek. 37). The prophet envisioned a valley full of bones, stripped of flesh and bleached in the sun. A more hopeless prospect for reanimation could scarcely be imagined. Nevertheless, God commanded him to prophesy that the bones should be revived, and as he did so, they were reclothed with flesh, "and stood up upon their feet, an exceeding great army" (37:10). The primary meaning of the vision was national restoration, not individual return from physical death. "Thus saith the Lord Jehovah: Behold, I will open your graves, and cause you to come up out of your graves, O my people; and I will bring you into the land of Israel. And ye shall know that I am Jehovah, when I have opened your graves, and caused you to come up out of your graves, O my people" (37:12-13).

The national application, however, must be viewed also from the perspective of God's total purpose for Israel. The nation was constituted expressly to provide a vehicle of revelation to the world at large, and to become the cradle for the Messiah. In Him the character and destiny of Israel would find its complete expression and fulfillment. The nation's common sufferings, joys, and triumphs would be epitomized in His experience, making its history one continuous prophecy of His significance for mankind.

The apparent ambiguity in the Old Testament prophecies was resolved by the interpretation supplied through the New Testament. If the Gospels afford a fair criterion of Jesus' teaching concerning Himself and the disciples' understanding of it, they certify that He was the key to the meaning of prophecy. Matthew repeatedly employed the phrase "that it might be fulfilled which was spoken by the prophet" to define the prophetic precedent of an event in Jesus' life. Some of these explanations seem irrelevant until one realizes that they do not demand correspondence of event to event so much as event to principle. A pertinent illustration is found in Hosea 11:1, "I . . . called my son out of Egypt." Matthew asserts that the descent of Mary and Joseph

into Egypt with the infant Jesus and their later settlement at
Nazareth fulfilled the prophecy (Matt. 2:13-15). A careful examination of the context in Hosea reveals no connection with an
individual but shows the text to be a figurative reminiscence of
the Exodus. The rise of the nation from obscurity, God's acknowledgment of its sonship, its testing in the wilderness, its
march to conquest, and its testimony to His goodness and power
were paralleled in the life of Jesus. Insofar as His career reca-
pitulates that of the nation, the Matthean interpretation is valid.
In this way the latent prophecies can be explained, and the New
Testament allusions become meaningful.

Interpretation of Old Testament Predictions

When Jesus first informed the disciples that He would rise
from the dead, they did not comprehend His meaning, but afterwards they recalled His words and "believed the scripture . . ."
(John 2:22). Though John, who recorded the incident, did not
identify any single Old Testament source, he implied that the
disciples should have understood Jesus' words immediately from
their knowledge of the sacred canon. The New Testament presupposes that the Law and the Prophets contained predictions,
obscure or unrecognized at first, but clarified later by the manifestation of Christ.

Jesus alluded to scriptural antecedents on several occasions.
The first instance appears in Mark. "And he began to teach
them, that the Son of man must suffer many things, and be
rejected by the elders, and the chief priests, and the scribes, and
be killed, and after three days rise again" (8:31). The verb translated "rise again" indicated that the resurrection was a necessary
element of the pattern which the coming Messiah should follow.

Another episode confirms this conclusion. Following the Transfiguration, Jesus cautioned His disciples not to announce the
event until He should have risen from the dead (Mark 9:9). The
disciples debated the meaning of His words, then inquired why
the scribes declared that Elijah's coming must precede the
Messiah. Jesus replied that both Elijah and the Messiah would

come, "as it is written" of them (Mark 9:12, 13; Mal. 4:5).

Jesus repeated the prediction at the commencement of the last journey to Jerusalem. Mark (10:32-34) does not mention His allusion to the Scriptures, but the Lukan parallel says, "Behold, we go up to Jerusalem, and all the things that are written through the prophets shall be accomplished unto the Son of man. For he shall be delivered up unto the Gentiles, and shall be mocked, and shamefully treated, and spit upon: and they shall scourge and kill him: and the third day he shall rise again. And they understood none of these things; and this saying was hid from them, and they perceived not the things that were said" (Luke 18:31-34). By the inclusion of the phrase, "the things that are written," Jesus connected the events of His Passion with the Old Testament. Luke's threefold comment shows that the disciples did not understand the significance of Jesus' words until after the event had transpired.

The relation of the resurrection to the Old Testament was most clearly established through Jesus' conversation with two disciples on the road to Emmaus: "O foolish men, and slow of heart to believe in all that the prophets have spoken! Behoved it not the Christ [Messiah] to suffer these things, and to enter into his glory? And beginning from Moses and from all the prophets, he interpreted to them in all the scriptures the things concerning himself" (Luke 24:25-27).

At the later appearance to the disciples in the upper room Jesus mentioned "the law of Moses, and the prophets, and the psalms" (Luke 24:44), reiterating the pronouncement that the Messiah must "rise again from the dead the third day" (24:46). The Lord indicated that the teaching was not confined to one period or to one stratum of revelation. The validity of Messianic prophecy rests on the authority of Jesus Himself.

Jesus' exposition of Scripture laid the foundation for apostolic teaching. Although the Gospels seldom identify His choice of texts, the apostolic sermons in Acts and occasional references in the Epistles afford a few clues. Their treatment of the Old Testament undoubtedly reflects His comments on the sources upon which He usually founded His interpretation of Messianic prophecy. A few examples will illustrate the important types or predictions of the resurrection that are recognized in the New Testament.

The Protevangelium

The germ of predictive prophecy from which subsequent revelation developed is the word that God spoke to the tempter on the occasion of man's initial sin: ". . . I will put enmity between thee and the woman, and between thy seed and her seed: he shall bruise thy head, and thou shalt bruise his heel" (Gen. 3:15). The imagery depicts a gardener encountering a venomous snake, which he destroys by crushing its head, but not before the snake has sunk its fangs into his heel. The serpent is killed; the gardener achieves his victory at the cost of enduring the agony of the poison in his own body. In similar fashion "the seed of the woman" will triumph over death by voluntarily submitting to it, and will bring redemption and freedom to the race.

The theme of a "seed" embodying the Messianic promise persists throughout the Old Testament. The genealogy of Genesis 5 may be called "the highway of the seed" because it records the generations through which God preserved the hope of deliverance. To Abraham God promised descendants as numerous as the stars of the heavens, who should retain permanent possession of the land (Gen. 15:1-5, 18). A later development was the covenant with David, which guaranteed the perpetuation of royal authority in "the seed of David" (II Sam. 7:12; Ps. 89:3, 4).

The metaphor of the "seed" by which the Old Testament described the nation of Israel or the posterity of David was applied to Christ by Paul. He interpreted "the seed of Abraham," a collective term, to mean the individual Christ (Gal. 3:16), in whom the Messianic purpose has been consummated. Before the synagogue at Antioch of Pisidia he equated the "sure blessings of David," Isaiah's phrase for the Davidic covenant (Isa. 55:3), with the resurrection of Jesus: "And as concerning that he raised him [Jesus] up from the dead, now no more to return to corruption, he hath spoken on this wise, I will give you the holy and sure blessings of David" (Acts 13:34). The enduring throne promised to David's Messianic Son presupposed superiority over the vicissitudes of fortune, including death.

The Sacrifice of Isaac

Recounting the heroic acts of faith, the writer of Hebrews connected the sacrifice of Isaac with the idea of resurrection. "By faith Abraham, being tried, offered up Isaac: yea, he that had gladly received the promises was offering up his only begotten son; even he to whom it was said, In Isaac shall thy seed be called: accounting that God is able to raise up, even from the dead; from whence he did also in a figure receive him back" (Heb. 11:17-19).

A comparison with the original account in Genesis (22:1-19) reveals several surprising features. The promises which God had given to Abraham centered in Isaac and would normally find their fulfillment through his life. If Abraham's descendants were to be multiplied as the stars of heaven (15:5), Isaac would have to survive long enough to marry and to have children, for his death would effectually close the succession on which the perpetuation of the seed depended. The command seemed to be a contradiction, for how could God consistently make a promise and then remove all possibility of fulfillment? Abraham was forced into the dilemma of disobeying God's word to retain the fulfillment of the promise, or else of relinquishing faith in His truthfulness. The only solution for the impasse would be obedience, based on the belief that God would restore Isaac from the dead.

Another interesting aspect of this account is that Abraham seemed to have possessed the requisite faith. Accompanied by two servants to the mountain of Moriah, where the sacrifice had been appointed, Abraham and Isaac left them behind to make the slow ascent. Parting from them, Abraham said, "Abide ye here with the ass, and I and the lad will go yonder; and we will worship, and come again to you" (22:5). These words could be interpreted as a subterfuge to conceal Isaac's prospective fate from the servants, but a fuller consideration of the context indicates otherwise. Abraham was confident that Isaac would return with him, because he believed that even if he died, God would restore him. His perfect confidence in the character and promises of God despite the inexplicable paradox of His command is expressed in his words to Isaac, "God will provide himself the lamb for a burnt offering . . ." (22:8).

Through this experience God was endeavoring to disclose to Abraham in pictorial form the meaning of the coming incarnation and atonement. The whole episode reveals a father who loves his only son; a son who is of one mind with the father; a willingness to surrender life itself that the father's purpose may be accomplished; the potential completion of the entire act of sacrifice; and the restoration of the son to life that he may carry out the full measure of the father's plan. Abraham on Mount Moriah participated in a dramatic projection of Calvary and the resurrection. Perhaps Jesus was alluding to this episode when He said, "Abraham rejoiced to see my day . . . and was glad" (John 8:56).

The Revelation to Moses

When God called Moses from tending the sheep of Jethro in the wilderness, He revealed Himself by saying, "I am the God of thy father, the God of Abraham, the God of Isaac, and the God of Jacob" (Exod. 3:6). Jesus repeated the declaration in His debate with the Sadducees (Mark 12:18-27), who attempted to prove by a question based on the levirate law of marriage (Deut. 25:5-10) that a resurrection would be absurd. Citing the hypothetical case of a woman who had been married successively to seven brothers in order to preserve children in the family line, they asked whose wife she would be in the age to come. By inference they concluded that there could be no resurrection; otherwise the law of God would have created a situation essentially immoral. Jesus informed them that the future life would not include marriage, then quoted the text from Exodus to clinch His argument. If God is the God of the living, the patriarchs

Abraham, Isaac, and Jacob must still be alive, and life after death is a reality.

Jesus interpreted the passage by the same method of inference that His opponents had used, and to their way of thinking His procedure was as legitimate as theirs. The important aspect is not the hermeneutic method by which He reached His conclusion, but the fact that He taught the possibility of resurrection on the basis of Old Testament revelation. His authority makes the conclusion valid.

The Exodus

Another prophecy may be found in the national experience of Israel. When Moses and Elijah appeared with Christ on the mount of Transfiguration, they spoke of His "exodus" which He should accomplish at Jerusalem (Luke 9:31). The term refers to His death, as a parallel in II Peter 1:15 indicates. It may, however, apply also to His Passion as a whole, in which case it would include the empty tomb and the ascension.

The Exodus of Israel was the redemption and resurrection of a nation (Exod. 12:1-41). Jacob and his sons had migrated into Egypt in time of famine. They settled in the land of Goshen, where their descendants remained until a king arose who enslaved them, making their lives miserable by repressive legislation and by forced labor. Finally God sent Moses, who united the people and instituted the Passover. In this feast the blood of a sacrificial lamb was sprinkled on the lintel and doorposts of each Israelite house. As the angel of death passed through the land of Egypt on his grim errand, the Israelites who had complied with the Passover regulations were spared, and marched out of Egypt to begin a new life. From the slavery of oppression and from the condemnation of death they crossed the Red Sea into a new liberty.

For Jesus the resurrection was an exodus from bondage. Having shared with mankind the oppressive limitations imposed by the consequences of sin, He passed through the waters of death and emerged triumphant. As the Israelites under Moses' leadership gained their freedom from Egypt's tyranny, so believers in Christ participate in Christ's triumph. John of Damascus caught this imagery in his hymn:

> Come, ye faithful, raise the strain
> Of triumphant gladness;
> God has brought His Israel
> Into joy from sadness.
> Loosed from Pharaoh's bitter yoke
> Israel's sons and daughters;
> Led them with unmoistened foot
> Through the Red Sea waters.

The Feast of the Firstfruits

The feasts of the Old Testament celebrated important events in the life of Israel. They were intended to remind the people of God's dealing as He worked out the process of their national redemption. The Passover recalled the deliverance from bondage and death in Egypt. Fifty days after the Passover came the Feast of the Wave-loaves, later known as Pentecost, when the bread from the new grain harvest was presented to God. The Feast of the Firstfruits (Lev. 23:10, 11) intervened between these two, on the first day after the Passover sabbath and three days after the sacrifice of the lamb, when a small sheaf of the first grain of the season was gathered and dedicated to God as a sample and pledge of the more abundant future harvest.

The Passover was a type of Christ, as Paul later affirmed, "For our passover also hath been sacrificed, even Christ" (I Cor. 5:7). Similarly the Feast of the Firstfruits prefigures His resurrection, because He is called "the firstfruits of them that are asleep" (I Cor. 15:20). The life of the seed springing from the dark cold earth demonstrates a vitality that death cannot repress. The parallelism seems inescapable.

The Psalms

Prophecies of Christ in the Psalms were mentioned by nearly all the writers of the New Testament. Paul, preaching in the synagogue of Antioch of Pisidia, quoted the second Psalm, "And we bring you good tidings of the promise made unto the fathers, that God hath fulfilled the same unto our children, in that he raised up Jesus; as also it is written in the second psalm, Thou art my Son, this day have I begotten thee" (Acts 13:32-33) .

Psalm 2 celebrates the elevation of a king to the throne of Israel, for he is seated upon the "holy hill" of Zion. The tributary kings of the Gentiles are on the verge of revolt, but God declares him to be His anointed and invests him with sovereignty over the nations. The Messianic character of this Psalm is established by Jesus' quotation in Matthew 22:41-45 to show that David called the Messiah "Lord."

The hinge of Paul's argument is the word "begotten," which he equated with the resurrection. One might naturally assume that it would refer to the birth of the Messiah, or that it would be a hint of the "eternal generation" of the Son who sprang from the being of the Father before all eternity. A careful examination of the Psalm will show, however, that the origin of the Son is not under discussion. "This day have I begotten thee" relates to the enthronement, not to birth. The Pauline interpretation is in keeping with the main thought, for the resurrection of Christ was God's seal of approval upon His ministry and was the beginning of His exaltation after the humiliation of Calvary. Christ "was declared to be the Son of God with power . . . by the resurrection from the dead" (Rom. 1:4). "Begotten" implies the possession of the very life of God, which is not subject to death.

The sixteenth Psalm was applied to the resurrection by both Peter (Acts 2:25-31) and Paul (13:35-37). Written in a time of comparative prosperity, it records David's aspirations for the future.

> I have set Jehovah always before me:
> Because he is at my right hand, I shall not be moved.
> Therefore my heart is glad, and my glory rejoiceth:
> My flesh also shall dwell in safety.
> For thou wilt not leave my soul to Sheol;
> Neither wilt thou suffer thy holy one to see corruption.
> Thou wilt show me the path of life:
> In thy presence is fulness of joy;
> In thy right hand there are pleasures for evermore.

Peter declared this Psalm to be a prediction of the Messiah because it could not apply strictly to David, whose tomb was a landmark in Jerusalem in the first century, and who had not been resurrected. His soul was still in Sheol, the abode of the spirits of the dead, and his flesh had gone down to corruption, literally, *the pit,* a term usually applied to the physical aspect of burial and dissolution. The "holy one" must therefore be David's heir and successor, the Messiah. The Psalm expresses personal faith, and the expectation of exaltation after death to the right hand of God.

A similar expression occurs in the forty-ninth Psalm.

> But God will redeem my soul from the power of Sheol:
> For he will receive me (Ps. 49:15).

Psalm 49 is not usually considered Messianic and may state only the general hope of the writer for deliverance from death. It does, however, define more exactly the Old Testament concept of the resurrection by contrasting the impersonal power of Sheol, the abode of the dead, with the personal redemption which God effects in a believer by "receiving" him. The Psalmist anticipates Jesus' promise: "I . . . will receive you unto myself; that where I am, there ye may be also" (John 14:3).

Peter also quoted from Psalm 118, one of the Songs of Ascent, customarily sung by pilgrims who went up to Jerusalem to celebrate the Passover. The Gospels, by associating the Psalm with the triumphal entry (Luke 19:38; Ps. 118:26), assert its prophetic connection with Christ. Peter used it to confirm the truth of the resurrection (Acts 4:10, 11).

> The stone which the builders rejected
> Is become the head of the corner (Ps. 118:22).

The imagery is borrowed from the construction of a building, perhaps from the erection of the Temple. The "cornerstone" may not have meant the inscribed block that modern buildings place at the corner of the foundation, but rather the keystone of the highest arch or the capstone of the dome. It would necessarily have an odd shape, which would be impossible to fit into any part of the structure except the one place for which it was de-signed. Christ was not accepted by the Jewish people because they could not fit Him into their theological system or into their political scheme. They rejected and crucified Him, but His resur-rection made Him the keystone of their national destiny.

The Prophets

In the writings of the prophets there are comparatively few significant references to life after death. One of the earliest and most striking is found in Hosea. "Come, and let us return unto Jehovah; for he hath torn, and he will heal us; he hath smitten, and he will bind us up. After two days will he revive us: on the third day he will raise us up, and we shall live before him" (Hos. 6:1-2). The prediction does not concern a personal experi-ence, but national revival after chastening. Nevertheless, Matthew's comment on Hosea 11:1, ". . . that it might be fulfilled which was spoken by the Lord through the prophet, saying, Out of Egypt did I call my son" (Matt. 2:15), applies the prophet's words to Messiah. If Hosea equates the nation with the Messiah, then perhaps Hosea 6:1-2 is also an allusion to His death and resurrection. The relation, however, is remote, for the prophet used the concept of resurrection figuratively to describe restora-tion after repentance.

The clearest prophetic source for redemption is the fifty-third chapter of Isaiah. "He was cut off out of the land of the living . . . And they made his grave with the wicked, and with a rich man in his death . . . when thou shalt make his soul an offering for sin, he shall see his seed, he shall prolong his days, and the pleasure of Jehovah shall prosper in his hand. . . . Therefore will I divide him a portion with the great, and he shall divide the spoil with the strong; because he poured out his soul unto death, and was numbered with the transgressors . . ." (Isa. 53:8, 9, 10b, 12). The prophet, speaking of the Servant, presents contrasting pictures of suffering and triumph. The two cannot be simultaneous; one must follow the other. In the given sequence the triumph follows the suffering, thereby implying a resurrection.

Certain specific statements support this inference. "He shall see his seed" assumes that the dead person will live to see his descendants or successors. A parallel in the New Testament speaks of "bringing many sons unto glory" (Heb. 2:10). "He shall prolong his days" implies that life will not be terminated by the sacrifice. "The pleasure of Jehovah shall prosper in his hand" declares that the resurrected Messiah will complete His divine commission.

The identity of the mysterious Servant is established by apostolic interpretation. To the Ethiopian eunuch, bewildered by Isaiah's veiled language, the evangelist Philip explained that the prophet was speaking of Jesus (Acts 8:28, 32-35). If He is the suffering Servant, He is also the Victor who will return from death to share His triumph with them.

The witness of the Old Testament, though shadowy and incomplete, presages a greater revelation in the person of the Messiah. He is the fulfillment of its types and the realization of its promises.

The Predictions of Jesus

Some of Jesus' comments have already been discussed in connection with the fulfillment of the Old Testament prophecies. He taught that His Messianic career had been planned in the mind of God from eternity and that He was following the divine pattern as it had been revealed in the Scriptures. He was encouraged and directed at crucial intervals by the guidance of the Holy Spirit, through whom He had been equipped for this task (Luke 4:18, quoting Isa. 61:1, 2). The resurrection was an essential part of His life, and as Jesus' ministry progressed He spoke with increasing definiteness concerning it.

The initial prediction was connected with the cleansing of the Temple, which John assigned to the first visit to Jerusalem. Jesus began His Messianic mission by sternly expelling the merchants who had made His Father's house into a bazaar. The priests naturally asked by what right He should take command of the Temple courts, of which they were the official custodians. What sign could He produce to substantiate His authority? He answered, "Destroy this temple, and in three days I will raise it up" (John 2:19).

Because Jesus did not explain the cryptic utterance, His enemies gave it an obvious but wrong interpretation. They assumed that He was speaking of the unfinished stone and wood building which Herod had been erecting for the last forty-six years. John, the author and the disciple closest to Jesus, adds the footnote that He was speaking of the temple of His body (2:21). The multitude did not understand Jesus' remark, nor did the disciples until they recalled it later. He indicated that He was already anticipating the Passion and was looking forward to the culminating "sign" of His career.

Although the Synoptics do not connect the resurrection with the cleansing of the Temple, they mention it in another setting. Shortly after the imprisonment of John the Baptist, when Jesus' ministry was approaching a crisis, the Pharisees challenged Him for a sign. He replied, "An evil and adulterous generation seeketh after a sign; and there shall no sign be given to it but the sign of Jonah the prophet: for as Jonah was three days and three nights in the belly of the whale; so shall the Son of man be three days and three nights in the heart of the earth" (Matt. 12:39-40). In this declaration Jesus maintained the same emphasis of a "sign" by comparing Himself with Jonah. On his mission to Nineveh the prophet was swallowed by the sea-monster, and three days later was disgorged safely on dry land. His miraculous preservation accredited him with the Ninevites. Jesus claimed to be greater than Jonah, because His experience would transcend Jonah's and would be proof of a higher authority.

Jesus' most definite predictions are grouped near the time of the Transfiguration. Matthew and Mark give a series of four, of which Luke parallels only two, possibly because he was endeavoring to avoid repetition. The four occasions are not the same, however, nor are the accounts careless reiteration. Each presents a different aspect of the subject.

The first, stated in almost identical terms by the three Synoptic Gospels (Matt. 16:21; Mark 8:31; Luke 9:22), follows immediately Peter's confession at Caesarea Philippi. Jesus had reached the

peak of His popularity and the cross was inevitable. Before He
could explain the impending crisis to His followers, He must be
sure of their acceptance of His claims and of their personal allegiance. When Simon Peter acknowledged Him as the Messiah,
the Son of the living God, Jesus was confident that they had
enough spiritual maturity to receive further disclosures. Mark's
comment, "And he spake the saying openly" (Mark 8:32), indicates that whereas Jesus had previously given hints of His death
and resurrection, He had not declared His intentions to the
public.

The disciples were shocked and bewildered by Jesus' announcement. If one may judge from Peter's rebuke, they were so scandal-
ized by the idea of suffering that they overlooked the allusion to
the triumph. It was not lost to Jesus' thinking, however, as the
next instance in the series shows.

About a week later, Jesus took Peter, James, and John into a
high mountain, where He was transfigured before them. To this
select group He revealed His inherent glory which had been laid
aside at the incarnation. As they descended from the mountain
afterwards, He instructed them to "tell the vision to no man,
until the Son of man be risen from the dead" (Matt. 17:9). Mark
(9:10) adds that "they kept the saying, questioning among themselves what the rising again from the dead should mean." The
concept of resurrection could not have been foreign to the disciples, for it was in Jesus' day a common tenet of Judaism (cf. John
11:24). The aspect that puzzled them was Jesus' application of
the principle to Himself, as if He would rise from the dead before
the last general resurrection. From this context it is plain that the
disciples did not foist this concept upon Jesus' career for the
purpose of making Him a supernatural character. The prediction was not their invention, but His revelation, which they remembered only when the event had given it meaning.

The third discourse, recorded by Matthew and Mark (Matt.
17:22, 23; Mark 9:30-32), does not vary greatly from the others,
but the occasion is different. According to Mark's account Jesus
and His disciples were already passing through Galilee on their
way to Jerusalem. The recorded reactions of the disciples seem

to indicate that they were slowly becoming aware of Jesus' intentions. Matthew says that they were "exceeding sorry"; Mark explains that "they understood not the saying, and were afraid to ask him." Like children who can feel emotional tension without being able to comprehend its causes or significance, the disciples sensed the gravity of the situation but had no clear idea of its full importance. They understood the meaning of His words, but not the meaning of the crisis.

The fourth reference appears in the narrative of the actual journey to Jerusalem (Matt. 20:17-19; Mark 10:32-34; Luke 18:31-33). Jesus spoke more explicitly than on the preceding occasions, but the disciples did not comprehend His purpose. James and John requested the foremost places of power in the kingdom, overlooking completely the prediction of imminent suffering (Matt. 20:20-28; Mark 10:35-45). Jesus reminded them forcefully that He had not come to receive homage, but to give His life as a sacrifice. Mark mentions the emotional confusion and fear of the disciples: "they were amazed; and they that followed were afraid" (Mark 10:32). Luke stresses their intellectual obtuseness: "they understood none of these things; and this saying was hid from them, and they perceived not the things that were said" (Luke 18:34).

Jesus' final allusion, "But after I am raised up, I will go before you into Galilee" (Matt. 26:32), was spoken just after leaving the upper room in Jerusalem. Although His impending betrayal and death weighed heavily upon Him, He anticipated the triumph. The undercurrent of His thinking was even more apparent in the discourses of John 14, 15, and 16, and in the prayer of John 17, where He petitioned the Father for a return to His preincarnate glory.

This recurrent series of pronouncements reveals that from the commencement of His ministry Jesus made the resurrection His objective. To the public He spoke of it in veiled words; to the disciples He expressed Himself openly. The historical fact was inextricably woven into the fabric of Jesus' life and teaching. The doctrinal aspect was developed more fully when the witnesses had opportunity to meditate on the event and to formulate the implications into an organized theology.

In several of the foregoing instances, Jesus stressed the detail that He would rise from the dead *on the third day* (John 2:19; Matt. 12:40, 16:21, 17:23, 20:19, and parallels). One of these, "he must . . . the third day be raised up" (Matt. 16:21), implies that the prescribed interval of time was not accidental. Acccording to Jesus' subsequent explanation to the disciples on the road to Emmaus (Luke 24:46) and the apostolic preaching (Acts 10:40; I Cor. 15:4) the three-day period was prophesied in the Scriptures.

Jesus' declaration created a hermeneutical puzzle, for there is no explicit statement in the Old Testament which connects His resurrection with a three-day period. There are, however, numerous allusions to "three days" or "the third day," which might be susceptible of figurative interpretation. The first of these belongs to the account of creation. "And God said, Let the earth put forth grass, herbs yielding seed and fruit-trees bearing fruit after their kind, wherein is the seed thereof, upon the earth: and it was so" (Gen. 1:11-13). The third day brought the first signs of life after the chaos and darkness from which the creation emerged.

The restoration of Isaac to his father took place on the third day after God had given the initial command that he should be offered as a sacrifice (Gen. 22:4). During that interval he was virtually dead to Abraham, and only after God had forbidden Abraham to slay him was Isaac truly alive in his father's sight.

When Pharaoh's private butler and baker were imprisoned, Joseph interpreted their dreams, promising release to the butler "within . . . three days" (Gen. 40:13). He was potentially under sentence of death but on the designated day was restored to his former position.

Joseph's brothers, upon their arrival in Egypt, were arrested on a charge of espionage and were remanded to prison. Undoubtedly they expected the worst, but after three days they were freed (Gen. 42:17, 18) and resumed their normal activities.

A somewhat different emphasis is given in Exodus 19:11. Moses announced to the people of Israel that they should prepare themselves to meet God, for He would manifest Himself "the third day" on Mount Sinai in the sight of the whole congregation. It became the day of revelation, when God's person and purposes were announced to His people, and when the objective of the deliverance from Egypt was disclosed. For Israel a new corporate life was beginning.

Among the allusions in the prophets there are only two texts which mention the third day. The promise of Hosea for revival (Hos. 6:2) is the sole instance which connects this time element with the concept of rising from the dead.[7] The final use of this phrase, occurring in the prophecy of Jonah (Jon. 1:17), is an incident in his biography rather than a topic of his preaching.[8] Aside from the fact that Jonah's obedience was reluctant, whereas Christ's was voluntary, there is a strong parallel between the two. Both were sacrificed for the safety of others; both were three days in darkness; and both were restored to a broader and more effective work for God by a miracle which confirmed their divine commission. Jesus Himself made the application of the analogy and stressed the chronological element (Matt. 12:39, 40).

Not one of these instances can be classed as a direct prediction of the Messiah. Since the New Testament rarely identifies the texts on which Jesus based His teaching, the interpreter cannot be certain of the precise sources. Nevertheless, the foregoing references must include at least the majority of those that are relevant.

The chief reason for laying emphasis on the three-day period may be found in the Jewish belief that the spirit did not finally leave the body until the fourth day, which marked the beginning of decomposition and ended the possibility of resuscitation. At the raising of Lazarus Martha protested against opening the tomb because he had been dead four days, and disintegration would have commenced already (John 11:39). Peter, in the sermon at Pentecost, remarked that Jesus' flesh saw no corruption (Acts 2:31), possibly because the time of His interment had not exceeded the limit.

One hesitates to ascribe any mystical significance to the number three, lest he lapse into the realm of fantasy. On the other hand, there are certain connotations of this number in Scripture that may affect its meaning. Dr. Wilbur M. Smith has observed that

[7] Cf. *supra*, p. 39.
[8] Cf. *supra*, p. 41.

the period of three days is connected frequently with the concept of darkness or punishment.[9] The plague of darkness in Egypt lasted three days (Exod. 10:22, 23). David was disciplined by a pestilence of three days' duration for his sin in numbering the people (II Sam. 24:13). Paul, blinded by the heavenly vision on the road to Damascus, was confined to his lodgings for three days until he was healed (Acts 9:9). Sometimes it was an interval of testing, as in the case of the Gibeonites, with whom Israel made a treaty after waiting three days (Josh. 9:16). Restoration was also associated with this period of time. Hezekiah was healed of illness and was able to worship in the Temple on the third day (II Kings 20:5-8). Crisis, too, was involved, for Esther appeared before the Persian king to intercede for her people on the third day (Esther 5:1).

Similarly, the darkness of the grave, the testing of Jesus' promises and of the faith of the disciples, the restoration of the Crucified to a place of power and of influence, and the crisis of the struggle of life and death came to a climax in His resurrection on the third day. At the very time when defeat would normally become apparent because of the physical dissolution of His body, Jesus returned to life. His insistence upon this precise interval adds weight to His words, "I lay down my life, that I may take it again" (John 10:17).

There is no duplicate of this phenomenon in classic pagan literature, nor is there any comparable instance of its association with resurrection. Only in the Old and New Testaments is the third day consistently related to the concept of a return from death; it is original with the Biblical revelation. In contrast to other religious teachers, who would not have dared to assert that they would die, and rise on a given day, Jesus plainly declared His intentions and fulfilled them to the astonishment of all His followers.

---

[9] Wilbur M. Smith, "The Third Day According to the Scriptures," *Sunday School Times*, March 24, 1928, pp. 187, 188.

III *The Proclamation*
in the Acts and Gospels

The historic resurrection of Jesus transformed predictions into reality and became the core of Christian preaching from Pentecost to the present day. Before the narrative of Jesus' ministry was reduced to written form, it was presented orally in the synagogues of the Jews and in the public forums of the Gentile cities. The book of Acts preserves in condensed and sometimes fragmentary fashion addresses delivered on strategic occasions, which provide a criterion for determining the importance of this message in the earliest stage of the church's growth.

An examination of the discourses reveals that the topic was the distinctive subject of Christian preaching, whether it were directed to one man or to a crowd, to Jews or to Gentiles. Preaching presupposed both predictive prophecy and material evidence. If the sermons recorded in Acts may be taken as a fair index of apostolic method, more stress was placed upon the personal and spiritual value of the resurrection than upon controversy over its historicity or credibility. In the Gospels also the homiletic motif is apparent, for the authors seek to lead their readers from initial interest in Jesus as a prophet and teacher to faith in Him as their Messiah.

The Preaching in Acts

The value of the sermons has been challenged on the ground that ancient writers not infrequently put into the mouths of their characters speeches fabricated to fit the man and the occasion. Such procedure was not considered dishonest; it was a conventional device of historians.[1] On the other hand, one cannot conclude that Luke manufactured the speeches simply because such procedure was customary. He had direct contact with many persons who had heard them, and, in the case of Paul, he could have obtained a digest from the speaker himself. One cannot fairly reject the content of these sermons as spurious even though they may be fragmentary. Differences in style and close affinities in content and vocabulary with acknowledged works of their reputed authors indicate that the Lukan reports are faithful. For instance, Luke did not profess to quote Peter's sermon at Pentecost in its entirety, for he said, "And with many other words he testified, and exhorted . . ." (Acts 2:40). His reputation for historical truthfulness is high, and it is unlikely that he would have misrepresented or falsified the speeches which he quoted.[2]

Twelve major addresses, covering the period from the day of Pentecost (c. A.D. 30) to the close of Paul's Caesarean imprisonment (c. A.D. 60), represent the progress of the gospel from Jerusalem to Rome. Its development can be traced by explanations designed to meet the varying needs of different types of audiences, or to elaborate the implications discernible to maturing Christians. In each stage of presentation the place of the resurrection is constant; it is never deprecated or ignored but occupies a prominent place.

The first sermons recorded in Acts were spoken by Peter in Jerusalem and were intended for Jewish hearers. Their main objective was to show that God had reversed the verdict which the national leaders had passed on Jesus. Peter drew a sharp

---

[1] T. Hinshaw, *New Testament Literature* (London: Allen and Unwin, Ltd., 1952). See p. 194.

[2] R. B. Rackham, *The Acts of the Apostles* (London: Methuen and Company, [1904], pp. xliii-xliv.

contrast between the Jewish attitude and the divine purpose. "Ye killed him; God raised him" is the constant refrain (2:23, 24; 3:14, 15; 4:10; 5:30) . The immediate reaction was a sense of guilt, resulting either in repentance (2:37) or in hostility (4:2, 18; 5:33). The audiences in Jerusalem, where the circumstances were best known, were neither skeptical nor indifferent. Whether or not they were ready to accept the conclusions that Peter drew, they did not impugn his basic statement as illusory.

The meaning of the resurrection was explained in terms of the immediate circumstances or topic of discussion. On the day of Pentecost it was the explanation for the coming of the Spirit (2:33) . After the healing of the lame man Peter asserted that the cure had been effected by faith in the name of the risen Lord (3:16), whose advent consummated the fulfillment of Old Testament prophecy, and was the summons to repentance (3:18, 19) . In the later defense before the Sanhedrin Peter reaffirmed this doctrine (4:10) and claimed that only in Christ could salvation be found. After the second public arrest of the apostles (5:17, 18) they were again put on trial before the Sanhedrin, and they repeated this identical defense: "The God of our fathers raised up Jesus, whom ye slew, hanging him on a tree. Him did God exalt with his right hand to be a Prince and a Saviour, to give repentance to Israel, and remission of sins. And we are witnesses of these things; and so is the Holy Spirit, whom God hath given to them that obey him" (Acts 5:30-32) .

The Petrine preaching of these early days in Jerusalem does not contain any broad development of latent theological implications. The appeal to the Jewish audience was simple and direct, being confined chiefly to the verification of Jesus' messiahship and the establishment of the national guilt in rejecting Him. Peter directed his remarks to Israel rather than to the Gentile world at large. Within this proclamation, however, lay the germ of all Christian preaching, for the Gentile Luke recorded it as part of his volume, which was intended to serve the needs of friends outside the fold of Israel.

The address of Stephen (Acts 7) did not mention the subject directly, but the following vision certainly implied it. Had Christ not risen, Stephen could not have seen Him standing at the right hand of God (7:56). The address itself assumed the fact, for it was essentially an elaboration of the first half of Peter's charge, "[Ye] killed the Prince of life" (3:15). Stephen, having reviewed the historical rejection of God's appointed leaders by the people of Israel, accused them of having betrayed and murdered the Messiah. For him the resurrection marked the end of one revelation and the beginning of another.

Stephen's speech was pivotal. Until this crisis the apostles and other believers had been worshiping in the synagogues or in the Temple and had combined the observances of Judaism with belief in the messiahship of Jesus. Stephen declared that God is not confined to temples (7:48), but that with the advent of Jesus a new revelation had begun. The message of life could not be restricted to any one race or ritual; it was destined to be a faith for all mankind.

The transition from Judaism to universal Christianity is indicated more by the trend of the narrative in Acts than by argumentation, although later it came to a crisis in the debate at the Council of Jerusalem (15:1-29). At the end of the first stage of apostolic preaching the gospel of the resurrection was accepted, but it had not been expanded into a theological system.

The persecution precipitated by Stephen's speech and the consequent dispersion of the church produced a new type of preaching. Of the four addresses which can be assigned to this period, one was spoken by Peter in the house of the Roman centurion, Cornelius (10:34-43), and the remaining three were given by Paul at Antioch of Pisidia (13:16-42), Thessalonica (17:1-3), and Athens (17:18, 22-32). Two of these, the first and fourth, were addressed to predominantly Gentile audiences; the other two were delivered in synagogues which some Gentile proselytes attended. No one of the four, with the possible exception of the speech before the Areopagus, was offered strictly as a defense, for each was designed to be an evangelistic sermon rather than a plea before a court. The four contain greater variety of appeal than Peter's early addresses, for they were directed to audiences located in cities widely distant from each other and varying in cultural background.

At Caesarea (10:34-43) Peter reiterated the basic theme of his previous preaching but added significant corollaries. One was the exclusiveness of the resurrection revelation. "God ... made [him] manifest, not to all the people, but unto witnesses that were chosen before of God, even to us, who ate and drank with him after he rose from the dead" (10:40-41).

Cornelius, a hard-headed Roman centurion, might have challenged Peter's statement because Christ had not been manifested publicly after He emerged from the tomb. The preacher forestalled the objection by affirming that Jesus appeared only to select but competent witnesses who could testify that He truly had risen. Their united testimony provided a foundation for the faith upon which the apostles built the superstructure of their theology.

A second corollary is the concept of judgment. Jesus was "ordained of God to be the Judge of the living and the dead" (10:42). By one sentence Peter established the fundamental eschatological framework of Christianity. Judgment implies human responsibility for ethical behavior and a goal toward which the entire universe moves under the direction of God. Jesus was not merely a wandering prophet whose epigrams had casual literary or moral virtue. The resurrection validated His claim to be the Son of God, whose words were an eternal criterion of spiritual and moral values. As He Himself said, "the word that I spake, the same shall judge him in the last day" (John 12:48). A new age of probation was being introduced, decisive in its character and final in its outcome. There could be no more tolerance of moral indifference, for every act would be scrutinized in the light of Christ's resultant authority. Judgment would take place not only through the process of history, as Israel had already experienced it, but also at a future crisis when the righteous and risen Son of the Father would confront both the dead and the living.

Since judgment would inevitably entail the doom of all men, for none is righteous, a provision for salvation is necessary. Peter had referred to it previously (Acts 4:12), but for Gentiles he made the teaching more explicit. "To him bear all the prophets witness, that through his name every one that believeth on him shall receive remission of sins" (10:43). This promise is the culmination of the history of the Old Testament and the focus of its prophetic message. The grace of God which had been revealed progressively in His providential dealings with Israel overflowed all national barriers and became available "to everyone that believeth." Universal blessing was assured by Christ's rising from the dead, which confirmed His authority to forgive sins (Mark 2:10), and which guaranteed His eternal competence to make His promises effectual (Heb. 7:25).

A similar presentation characterized Paul's initial address to the Jews in the synagogue at Antioch of Pisidia. Like Peter, he followed the historical and prophetic interpretation with the theological application that through Christ forgiveness of sins was guaranteed. He added one further qualification, *"and by him every one that believeth is justified from all things, from which ye could not be justified by the law of Moses"* (Acts 13:39, italics ours). Paul carried the argument farther than Peter; not only does he say that forgiveness is available through faith in Christ, but in addition he states that the law is inadequate to justify the sinner. In that sentence lies the germ of the entire Pauline theology of justification by faith, which was a reversal of the rabbinic theology of salvation by works. Justification, however, is through "the man" whom God raised from the dead. One may fairly deduce that the resurrection was the beginning of Paul's revolutionary idea, and that the few words quoted from his sermon in Pisidian Antioch may have marked the inception of the total complex of theology appearing in his epistles.

The brief account of Paul's sermons in the synagogue of Thessalonica (17:2-3) gives no extended review of content but does outline his procedure. He reasoned that, according to the Scriptures, Messiah must suffer and rise again from the dead, and that Jesus of Nazareth was identical with the promised Messiah. Both ideas were disputed, for Jewish theologians of Paul's day had no concept of a suffering Messiah and were unlikely to accept the repulsive doctrine of one that had been crucified. Furthermore, the emotional reaction against the historical person would prejudice them more deeply against accepting His claims. Nevertheless, Paul's evidence was sufficiently cogent to induce a number of Jews and proselytes to commit themselves to the new faith. Once he had established the continuity between the Old Testament prophecy and the life of Jesus via the resurrection, it was possible to inaugurate an entirely new system of theology.

Paul utilized a different approach in his speech before the Areopagus in Athens (17:16-32). Since he was addressing philosophers rather than students of the Old Testament Scriptures, he began with natural theology. Taking his cue from an altar inscribed "To An Unknown God," he skillfully presented the transcendent Creator who could not be confined to any of the temples that filled the city. Paul emphasized the ethical duty of man to God and the certainty of judgment on the discharge of that duty. The inevitability and the finality of divine decision were assured by the resurrection of Jesus, whom God had appointed to be the judge.

The Athenian reaction of polite scorn was normally to be expected, because Greek thought allowed no place for the reconstitution of the physical body (17:32). Paul, however, adhered rigidly to this fact as the basis of his faith, even though he knew it would bring him into disfavor with the philosophers. His assurance of moral values and of cosmic purpose was founded on the supreme manifestation of divine power, which revealed the eternal justice and authority of God.

The last group of addresses were the apostle's replies to formal accusations before a court. Although they may not represent his usual sermonic style, they contain the substance of his faith, compressed into small compass to answer his judges concisely.

The first hearing was conducted by the Sanhedrin, the same body that had tried Peter and John. Because of the relentless prejudice against him, Paul recognized that any attempt to defend himself against his accusers would be futile. He adopted the stratagem of creating dissension in the ranks of his enemies by declaring, "Brethren, I am a Pharisee, a son of Pharisees: touching the hope and resurrection of the dead I am called in question" (23:6). His motives for interjecting a controversial issue were not unmixed, for he wanted to escape from the trap into which his enemies had thrust him. At the same time he attempted a sincere and vigorous defense of his faith. Paul was not magnifying a side issue solely to divert the attention of the council from himself; he was rather emphasizing the principle at stake.

At the second hearing, before Felix, the Roman governor, Paul repeated the reason for his behavior and beliefs. "But this I confess unto thee, that after the Way which they call a sect, so serve I the God of our fathers . . . having hope toward God, which these also themselves look for, that there shall be a resurrection both of the just and unjust" (24:14, 15).

In this short speech Paul confined himself to generalities, since the hearing involved only the high priest and Felix, neither of whom would have appreciated a dissertation on theology. He claimed that he had not deviated from Israel's hope for a resurrection, both of the righteous and of the wicked. He made no direct reference to the risen Christ, but if the principle be admitted, the instance could not logically be rejected. This truth was the focal theological issue of his controversy with Judaism.

Paul's insistence was not arbitrary or subjective. When Festus succeeded to the governorship of Palestine two years later and reopened Paul's case to clear the court docket left by his predecessor, the same question recurred. At the informal hearing before Agrippa, Festus introduced the prisoner by declaring that the accusations against him concerned "one Jesus, who was dead, whom Paul affirmed to be alive" (25:19). Irrespective of whether Festus believed in the resurrection or not, he understood the question to concern the specific historic instance of Jesus' reputed return from death. Paul subsequently confirmed Festus' impression by the narration of his conversion, concluding with a defense. "Having therefore obtained the help that is from God, I stand unto this day testifying both to small and great, saying nothing but what the prophets and Moses did say should come; how that the Christ must suffer, and how that he first by the resurrection of the dead should proclaim light both to the people and to the Gentiles" (26:22-23).

The total argument might be summarized as follows: Raising the dead is not impossible with God, and therefore the resurrection of Jesus is not excluded on a priori grounds; the objective appearance of the glorified Christ on the Damascus road transformed his career; and the historic fact was anticipated by the predictions of the prophets and of the law. The appeal to Agrippa to believe the prophets thus became a challenge to accept the proposed thesis and to commit himself to Paul's side of the hearing (26:27).

Festus' impulsive interruption, "Paul, thou art mad," and Agrippa's sarcastic scorn, "With but little persuasion thou wouldest fain make me a Christian," showed that neither man took the prisoner seriously. They dismissed Paul's beliefs as fantasy and adjudged him to be a harmless fanatic. He, however, made the doctrine central in his personal experience, and basic to his preaching.

The last allusion to the resurrection in the book of Acts was Paul's oblique reference in his message to the Jewish community in Rome. He introduced himself by saying, "because of the hope of Israel I am bound with this chain" (28:20). From a comparison with his words to Agrippa, "And now I stand here to be judged for the hope of the promise made of God unto our fathers," and, "Why is it judged incredible with you, if God doth raise the dead?" (Acts 26:6, 8), one may deduce that the "hope of Israel" is the resurrection, and that it becomes the channel of divine blessing for both Jews and Gentiles.

The discourses in Acts, whether public or private, indicate that this doctrine was the central tenet of the new faith. Christianity did not evolve from an accidental combination of Jesus' teachings with Jewish ethic and temple ritual but was the spontaneous outgrowth of the overwhelming fact that Christ had risen. The dynamic of this unique event produced the church and inspired its distinctive message.

The Preaching in the Gospels

The presentation of Christian truth in Acts is necessarily brief and fragmentary. In order to include the history of thirty years' missionary endeavor within the limits of one scroll, the author could not reproduce addresses extensively. The four Gospels are

a more satisfactory source for early Christian preaching. Apart
from the question whether they are based upon oral tradition or
upon documentary sources, they were obviously written to perpetuate the essential message concerning the Lord Jesus Christ. His
advent, career, teaching, death, and resurrection are the principal
topics because they formed a total complex directly related to the
spiritual needs and welfare of those for whom the Gospels were
written.

As the story of Jesus was repeated, different phases were emphasized. Luke, who stated explicitly both his motive and his method,
directed his Gospel to Theophilus to confirm his confidence in the
truths which he had already learned by oral transmission (Luke
1:1-4). John's purpose was to establish his readers' belief in Christ
(John 20:30, 31). Mark calls his writing "The beginning of the
gospel of Jesus Christ" (Mark 1:1), and Matthew introduces his
work as "The book of the generation of Jesus Christ, the son of
David, the son of Abraham" (Matt. 1:1). For each of these
Gospels, diverse in content and in purpose, the resurrection is the
climax.

For an adequate comprehension of meaning, the Gospels must
be studied individually, since their approach varied with the
didactic purpose of each.

Mark presented the resurrection as the explanation and goal of
Jesus' active life. He divided his biographical sketch into short
segments of irregular length, each of which pertained to a different geographical location. Beginning with the baptism at the
Jordan (Mark 1:9), he traced the progress of Jesus' ministry by
successive episodes of teaching and healing to its climax in the
retirement to Caesarea Philippi (8:27). There Jesus appealed to
the disciples for their verdict on His person, "But who say ye
that I am?" When Simon Peter voiced his confession, "Thou art
the Christ [Messiah]" (8:29), Jesus enjoined them not to pub-
licize His claims. From that time He began to teach them that
He would suffer and die, and would then rise again (8:31). Although these words were spoken exclusively to the disciples, for
Mark distinguished sharply between them (8:27) and the multitude (8:34), they introduced a new element into the presentation

of the Lord's person. The period of popularity had passed, and the suffering of the cross began to loom before Him. Tragedy, however, was not the end of His mission. The successes and the sufferings alike found their completion in the triumph of "the third day."

The Transfiguration which followed shortly after the revelation at Caesarea Philippi was closely related to this theme (9:2-10). Some scholars have suggested that it is a misplaced resurrection appearance.[3] To regard it as a preview of the glorified Christ in His kingdom is a better alternative (9:11). His appearance in a luminous body, accompanied by Moses and Elijah, was undoubtedly the means that Jesus utilized to prepare the disciples for the shock of the cross. His admonition to say nothing about the incident until He rose from the dead excited their curiosity and stimulated speculation. Since there is no record that Jesus explained His allusion, the disciples probably did not interrogate Him further. "Questioning among themselves" (9:10) implies that they hesitated to press Him for further information. The concept, however, was firmly lodged in their memory and may have provided the key by which John, one of their number, realized the significance of the empty tomb.

Overshadowed by the threat of impending death, Jesus seems to have been strangely preoccupied and aloof. The fate of John the Baptist had depressed His spirit, for it presaged His own end. On the last journey through Galilee He deliberately avoided publicity (9:30) and kept telling the disciples that He would fall a prey to His enemies in Jerusalem, but that He would afterwards rejoin them (9:31).

Jesus made the final allusion to His resurrection when He and the disciples were approaching Jerusalem prior to the Passion week. "And they were on the way, going up to Jerusalem; and Jesus was going before them: and they were amazed; and they that followed were afraid. And he took again the twelve, and began to tell them the things that were to happen unto him, say-

---

[3] See C. E. Carlston, "Transfiguration and Resurrection," *Journal of Biblical Literature*, LXXX (1961), 233-240. Carlston's defense of this view is not convincing.

ing, Behold, we go up to Jerusalem; and the Son of man shall
be delivered unto the chief priests and the scribes; and they shall
condemn him to death, and shall deliver him unto the Gentiles:
and they shall mock him, and shall spit upon him, and shall
scourge him, and shall kill him; and after three days he shall
rise again" (10:32-34).

The unusual silence of Jesus puzzled and frightened the disciples. Instead of talking with them freely He retreated within
Himself, walking a few paces ahead of them and paying little
attention to their comments. Finally He reiterated the prediction
of His death and again reproved them for their selfish aspirations.

Mark's motive for recording these instances seems to have been
a desire to put the cross in its proper perspective. The inevitability
of rejection weighed heavily upon the Master. The disciples did
not comprehend the circumstances, and they tended to dismiss
His predictions as idle fears or as improbable of fulfillment because He possessed miraculous power. Mark, contemplating the
words in retrospect, endeavored to show that the resurrection was
the climax of the divine plan.

The disclosures of the Saviour's purpose introduce the reader
to the eternal quality of His person. Any astute man, surrounded
by unscrupulous enemies and conscious of their determination to
destroy him, might foretell the mode and the approximate time of
his death, but could he predict that he would rise from the dead?
If he made such an assertion, who would believe him? And if any
did believe him, could they maintain their faith if he failed to
substantiate the claim? Jesus' language contains no trace of hopeless tragedy or of futile despair; on the contrary, He took for
granted that He would triumph over His enemies.

Two aspects of the ending of Mark's Gospel confirm this impression. One is the angel's word, "He goeth before you into
Galilee: there shall ye see him, as he said unto you" (16:7). Jesus
had previously announced at the time of His betrayal that He
would rise (14:28), and would meet His disciples in Galilee. They
had good reason to expect a future reunion, but the present ending of the Gospel leaves the thought incomplete, for it omits any
reference to Galilee. If, as some suppose, Mark terminated his

narrative at 16:8 with the words "for they were afraid," he may have purposely left the question open because the story of the living Christ merged with the continuing experience of the apostolic preachers, whose witness provided the logical sequel.

The authenticity of the last twelve verses is dubious since they do not appear in the most ancient manuscripts and are not noted by the earliest commentators. If genuinely Markan, they are probably a postscript which was added later for the benefit of those who had no contact with living witnesses. In any case, they doubtlessly preserve an ancient tradition which accords with the teaching of the rest of the Gospels. They do not alter the main presentation of the resurrection in the other accounts but confirm the impression that the doctrine was dominant in the preaching of the church.

The basic framework of Matthew's Gospel is almost identical with that of Mark. The differences lie chiefly in the use of available information. Matthew offers fuller explanation of the resurrection, employing it as one of the proofs of Jesus' messiahship. Answering the query of John the Baptist's disciples whether He were the Messiah whom John anticipated, Jesus said, "Go and tell John the things which ye hear and see: the blind receive their sight, and the lame walk, the lepers are cleansed, and the deaf hear, and the dead are raised up, and the poor have good tidings preached to them" (Matt. 11:4-5). Power over death was included among the signs which verified His authority.

In replying to the Pharisees' request for a "sign" (12:39, 40), Jesus likened Himself to Jonah, who returned to life after three days and three nights in the belly of the great fish. The illustration reflects the growing interest in a parallelism between Jesus and the Old Testament. Undoubtedly He originated the comparison, but the homiletic practice of relating His career to the divine action chronicled in the prophets may account for the preservation of the simile. Its typology suggested that, like Jonah, He would voluntarily give His life for the safety of others, and that His greatest ministry would follow the three-day parenthesis of death.

In other predictive passages (16:21; 17:9, 22, 23; 20:18, 19; 26:2)

Matthew connected the event with the time schedule of Jesus' life. "From that time began Jesus to show unto his disciples, that he must go unto Jerusalem, and suffer many things of the elders and chief priests and scribes, and be killed, and the third day be raised up" (16:21). The repeated forecasts of death and resurrection disclosed the purpose of Jesus and dominated His teaching during the last year of His life. They marked the stages of progress from Peter's great confession of faith in His messiahship to the climax of the cross. Evidently Matthew desired to impress upon his reader that the denouement of Jesus' career was as important as His discourses.

Matthew's chief divergence from Mark appears in the narrative concerning the Easter morning. Both agree that the women visited the tomb, and that an angel[4] informed them of Jesus' departure, announcing that He would meet the disciples in Galilee (Matt. 28:6, 7; Mark 16:6, 7). The difference lies in the reaction. Matthew declares, "they departed quickly from the tomb with fear and great joy, and ran to bring his disciples word" (Matt. 28:8). Mark adds an explanation: "they . . . fled from the tomb; for trembling and astonishment had come upon them: and they said nothing to any one; for they were afraid" (Mark 16:8).

Enslin claims that the Gospels are contradictory because Mark stresses the absolute silence of the women, whereas Matthew conveys the impression that they left the tomb with the avowed purpose of announcing the good news that Jesus had risen.[5] Enslin overlooks the obvious truth that the episode at the tomb would have remained unknown had not the women reported it to somebody. Mark means that they did not tell anyone apart from the disciples, for they had a commission to discharge and would be reluctant to discuss their experience with unsympathetic listeners. They would not dare to publish what they had witnessed, either because they would be regarded as religious fanatics or because their presence at the tomb would be a cause for suspicion of a plot.

---

[4] Mark's Gospel says, "a young man."

[5] Morton S. Enslin, "And That He Hath Been Raised," *Jewish Quarterly Review*, XLIII (1952-53), 29.

The apologetic purpose of Matthew shaped his account of the resurrection. The appearances of the angel and Jesus to the women asserted the supernatural character of the event, and the explanation of bribing the guard was evidently intended to correct a falsehood that had been widely circulated in the society to which Matthew and his readers belonged. His Gospel epitomizes the explanation given to Gentile groups that derived their initial impressions of Jesus from Jewish contacts. Matthew wished to free his readers from the misinformation circulated by the Jewish hierarchy and to clarify the true prophetic relation between Jesus and the promises of the Old Testament.

According to this Gospel, the appearances of Jesus were not the terminus of His career but were the beginning of a new stage. Jesus commanded that the message of the resurrection should be preached to "all the nations" (Matt. 28:19), or, as the phrase could be rendered, to "all the Gentiles." On this truth He founded His authority and made it the mainspring of the entire missionary enterprise.

The majority of the pertinent passages in the Gospel of Luke parallel those in Matthew and Mark and contribute no new information to the common stock, but there are a few significant additions revealing the author's interest in this doctrine.

When Jesus criticized the selfish behavior of guests at a feast, He suggested that His host should not invite only friends of equal social status but also the poor, the blind, and the crippled, who could not return the favor. Recompense for this generosity, He asserted, would be given at "the resurrection of the just" (Luke 14:14). The common ground of understanding between Jesus and His Jewish host would be the general Pharisaic belief, which Jesus endorsed and made the chief motive for charity. Luke's inclusion of the teaching assumes that the concept was perpetuated in the church and was a vital element in early doctrine.

Luke alone records Jesus' story of the rich man and Lazarus, the beggar. Whether this narrative should be interpreted as a parable, or whether Jesus was proffering a literal description of the unseen world, its final line reveals His belief in a return from death—and possibly is premonitory of His own experience.

"And he [Abraham] said unto him [the rich man], If they hear not Moses and the prophets, neither will they be persuaded, if one rise from the dead" (16:31). Jesus cherished no illusion that His resurrection would persuade all men of His authority. If in the period when the appearances were still verifiable by eyewitnesses their reality was disbelieved, how much more incredible would they seem in later years? Luke's quotation possibly reflected the current disbelief which he and his colleagues encountered.

Luke's chief contribution is the story of the journey to Emmaus. He could easily have obtained the details from Cleopas, who was one of the principals in the episode. The author's interest may have been prompted by the relation of Jesus' teaching to the Old Testament Scriptures. He intimated that the Stranger's two companions possessed full knowledge of the events which preceded the interview, but that they were unable to comprehend either the reason for His suffering or the phenomenon of the empty tomb. The facts were incontrovertible, but their understanding was inadequate.

There may have been other persons who were equally bewildered. They might acknowledge the reality of the empty tomb, but they were unsure of its meaning. Astute minds had already begun to speculate on the miracle involved. Had Jesus really risen as the apostles asserted, or had the body been stolen, as the Jewish authorities averred? The writer sought to show from Jesus' own testimony that the entire Passion was predicted in the Old Testament and was a part of God's design (24:27, 32, 44, 45). His repeated emphasis is an introduction to the literary presentation of apostolic preaching in Acts. The "certainty" which he wished to inculcate in Theophilus (1:4) was based at least partially on Christ's fulfillment of prophecy and upon His interpretation of the Old Testament teaching concerning Himself. Luke developed this aspect more than did Mark, who contented himself with merely recounting the facts, and more than Matthew, who specialized in the content of the teaching rather than in its framework.

Theophilus belonged to the cultured stratum of Roman society. His title, "most excellent" (1:3), may imply that he was a government official. If so, he was accustomed to travel and was familiar with the cults and beliefs of many lands. He would probably have regarded their extravagant legends concerning gods and goddesses as either superstitious or meaningless. The subjects of these legends had lived in the indefinite past, and their deeds could not be verified by acceptable proof. The converse was true of Jesus, for He was a contemporary of Theophilus' older Christian friends, and His numerous miracles were amply attested by eyewitnesses. The resurrection, which was the crowning wonder, was not only a historic fact established by external testimony; it was evidence that Jesus was unique. Theophilus' acceptance of His claims would be tantamount to an acknowledgment that He was different from the cult deities of the ancient world that belonged to the realm of imagination. Jesus, on the other hand, was a person whose human relations could be traced and whose impact upon His generation could not be denied.

The Gospel of John associated the resurrection directly with the theme of eternal life. The incarnation was a manifestation of God in human surroundings, the coincidence of time and eternity. John did not minimize the material aspects of Jesus' life, but he used select instances of His action and teaching to illustrate the principle that "In him was life; and the life was the light of men" (John 1:4). A comparison of the content of John with that of the Synoptic Gospels reveals that the peculiarly Johannine sections of text frequently consist of elaboration upon situations which the Synoptics have described. John assumed that his readers were acquainted with the general outline of gospel narrative and devoted his efforts to explaining more fully the One of whom it spoke.

According to the Fourth Gospel, eternal life and Christ are synonymous. The Father endowed the Son with life in Himself, which He in turn could impart to others (5:26; 10:10, 18). The impartation involved the new birth, a transformation of the character and will of the individual concerned (3:5-15), and was destined to reach its climax in the resurrection at the last day (5:25, 28, 29; 6:40, 44). Jesus identified Himself completely with this power when He said, "I am the resurrection, and the life: he that believeth on me, though he die, yet shall he live; and whosoever liveth and believeth on me shall never die" (11:25-26).

The raising of Lazarus illustrated vividly the foregoing promise. Jesus' delay in responding to the announcement of Lazarus' death had plunged Mary and Martha into deep discouragement. When Jesus finally arrived at Bethany they had relinquished all hope of restoration because four days had elapsed since the burial (11:39). Jesus assured them that their brother would rise again and challenged them to accept His word in spite of contradictory circumstances. His command, "Lazarus, come forth" (11:43), resuscitated the inert body by the impact of divine might and was a foretaste of the last summons that will marshal the dead before His judgment seat. The resurrection is the culminating manifestation of the life of God in a world of death.

John linked the resurrection closely with belief. When the Jews demanded proof of Jesus' authority to expel the merchants from the sacred courts of the Temple, He replied, "Destroy this temple, and in three days I will raise it up" (2:19). His enemies erroneously assumed that His cryptic remark concerned Herod's Temple, which after forty-six years was still in process of construction. They dismissed His statement as irrelevant or foolish; He had merely confused them. They recalled His words, however, and misused them when they charged Him with disloyalty at His trial before the Sanhedrin (Matt. 26:61). In an explanatory footnote John adds that He was speaking of His body, and that after the resurrection His disciples remembered His prediction, and believed both the Scriptures and His word. The footnote implies that one must view Jesus' life in the perspective of a mature faith in order to evaluate it correctly.

Prior to the resurrection the disciples regarded Jesus as a prophet with a message from God (John 4:19; 6:14; 7:40; 9:17), or as a potential king who could provide economic security and political independence for their nation (6:15). The Master, however, made a greater claim, for He promised that His obedient followers would live forever (8:51). Replying to the indignant protest of His opponents, who charged Him with sacrilege, He elevated Himself above the prophets when He declared, "Before

Abraham was born, I am" (8:58). Using the present tense of the verb *to be,* He asserted His eternal existence. By rising from the dead He confirmed this claim, and validated retroactively both His own promises and the faith of His followers.

In agreement with the Synoptic tradition the author unquestionably accepted the objectivity of the resurrection, but he did not represent it solely as a miraculous event, never to be repeated and dissociated from the normal currents of life. He interpreted it in terms of its effect on individuals, and showed that it imparted new courage and hope to those who witnessed and believed it. On the foundation of the external historical reality they built the assurance of Christ's continuing participation in their activities and His sovereignty over their destinies.

During Jesus' final conversation with the disciples before the betrayal, He promised to rejoin them after His death. "Yet a little while, and the world beholdeth me no more; but ye behold me: because I live, ye shall live also" (14:19). Later He became more explicit, "A little while, and ye behold me no more; and again a little while, and ye shall see me" (16:16). His language seemed ambiguous; it might describe either the ascension and second coming or His immediate return after death. The second alternative is probably the correct interpretation, for He explained that on the occasion of His departure His followers would lament, while the world would rejoice, but that their sorrow would be turned into joy. The resurrection became a standard of progress for the disciples. Not only could they refer to it later as the proof of Jesus' claims and the vindication of their faith, but also they could consider it a harbinger of their own victory over death.

The political and social aspects of prophecy are not discussed in the Fourth Gospel, which maintains a complete silence concerning the future of Israel and the church. Johannine eschatology is largely ethical and personal, emphasizing the ultimate relation of the individual to Christ. The language of John's First Epistle summarizes his viewpoint: "We know that, if he shall be manifested, we shall be like him; for we shall see him even as he is" (I John 3:2).

Jesus' final challenge (John 21:19) was given subsequent to the resurrection. When He first gathered His disciples, they expected the immediate establishment of the Messianic kingdom. His death crushed their hopes, but His subsequent appearance renewed the prospect for further development of His plans. Without defining His objective, Jesus commanded the disciples to follow Him. The resurrection became the basis of their confidence for a greater venture than the initial call to discipleship had involved. His invisible leadership, mediated by the Holy Spirit, would be the key to their future.

The conclusion of the Gospels marks an advance in the apostolic preaching concerning the resurrection. Whereas the earliest addresses reported in Acts stress the pivotal event upon which hinged the acceptance or rejection of Jesus' messiahship, the Gospels magnify the climactic reversal of fate which distinguished Him from all other religious leaders. The uniqueness of His person stimulates an analytic contemplation of His claims. The theology and ethics of the Epistles therefore spring naturally from an attempt to evaluate the risen Lord, who, as Paul said, was "declared to be the Son of God with power . . . by the resurrection of the dead" (Rom. 1:4).

IV *A Developing Theology*

The epistolary literature of the New Testament was composed by the apostles of Christ for the missionary churches which they had founded or in which they had ministered. The correspondence was evoked by the problems which Christians encountered in coping with legalistic Judaism and eclectic paganism. Converts drawn from both of these backgrounds sought answers to the theological and ethical questions raised by the conflict of the gospel with their former religions, and expected the preachers to resolve their difficulties. For this reason the preponderance of apostolic writing is directed toward specific problems rather than toward a systematic presentation of Christian theology. With few exceptions the Epistles resemble dialogues rather than lectures. They reveal the pattern of Christian thought by the presuppositions which were taken for granted both by the writer and the readers.

The Epistles mark an advanced stage of Christian faith, for they contain the application of the basic principles of the gospel to the needs of a living and growing church. Their authors assume a knowledge of the deeds and teachings of Christ recounted in the Gospel narratives, since these facts had been widely disseminated through the initial preaching. Upon this current knowledge the apostolic teachers built Christian ethics and apologetics.

In literary sequence, the Epistles antedated the Gospels. As long as the eyewitnesses lived, the church depended more upon oral testimony than upon written record for its knowledge of Jesus' life and teachings. Emergencies in the Christian communities, however, necessitated immediate instruction, evoking the intervention by letter that created the apostolic writings. These documents, therefore, explain the implications of the fundamental facts of Christian truth and apply them to the creed and conduct of the church. They embody the authoritative statement of the significance of Christ for the believer and for the world.

Chief among the facts about Christ is the resurrection. Numerous allusions reveal how thoroughly the concept became integrated with Christian theology, for almost every aspect of spiritual life is defined by its relationship to the crowning event of the Saviour's life.

The Pauline Epistles

Among the preachers of the apostolic age, Paul was the most influential. Although Peter, James, John, and others proclaimed the same message concerning Christ and created a literature of their own, Paul excelled them as a thinker and a preacher, so that the theological structure of the Christian faith originated primarily with him. The thirteen extant Epistles attributed to Paul comprise his total writing. Since most of them deal with theological or moral exigencies, no one of them presents a complete picture of his theology. It is impossible to reconstruct the entirety of the apostle's original Christian preaching from any single Epistle, but one can recover its general content from a combination of the main ideas given by the group. The cardinal tenets of Christian doctrine which Paul himself illustrated or stressed belonged to the comprehensive body of truth which the church proclaimed. His letters include occasional references to the substance of the message which he preached in pioneer territory. Paul epitomized the substance of his message in his first letter to the Corinthian church. "For I delivered unto you first of all that which also I received: that Christ died for our sins according to the scriptures; and that he was buried; and that he hath been raised on the third day according to the scriptures; and that he appeared . . ." (I Cor. 15:3-5a). He concluded this capsule statement with the words "So we preach, and so ye believed" (15:11). He claimed that his gospel was accepted by the entire church (Gal. 2:6-10) and that there was no distinction between him and the other preachers, except that his ministry was directed chiefly to the Gentiles, whereas theirs was for the Jews.

The period of Paul's literary activity covers nearly twenty years, beginning with the expansion of the missionary movement from the Gentile city of Syrian Antioch in A.D. 48, and extending to his final imprisonment and execution in Rome not later than A.D. 68. In these two decades he completed an itinerant ministry that extended to southern Asia Minor, Macedonia, Achaia, Illyricum, and even Rome itself. He built a series of active churches in the heart of the Roman empire that established Gentile Christianity and created a pattern for its subsequent growth. The Epistles are an index of the content of his message and of the unfolding of theology based upon the revelation of Christ.

Among these writings Romans is perhaps the broadest in scope. Written as a substitute for a personal visit which was precluded by the necessity of taking a contribution to the church in Jerusalem, Paul made the epistle a comprehensive statement of the plan of salvation. He discussed the nature of man's sin, God's provision of redemption in Christ, and the steps by which man can be reconciled to God and can attain holiness and power.

In this soteriological scheme the resurrection occupies a prominent place. It is initially the mark of Christ's divine sonship, for he "was declared to be the Son of God with power, according to the spirit of holiness, by the resurrection of the dead" (Rom. 1:4). Paul, in presenting Christ as a redeemer for men, was obligated to prove His authority, for without divine recognition He could not act as the mediator of God's revelation, nor could He make atonement for man before God. The genuineness of Jesus' humanity was demonstrated by His becoming subject to death; the power of His deity was manifested by His rising from the dead. The crowning miracle was the foundation of apostolic authority, because it gave to the Christian message a unique fusion of the historical and the supernatural in one event.

The same principle is involved in the introduction to Galatians, where Paul declared that he was "an apostle not from men, neither through man, but through Jesus Christ, and God the Father, who raised him from the dead" (Gal. 1:1). Confidence in the verity of the gospel confirmed by the resurrection enabled him to face a hostile world with courage and zeal. He could begin his theological system with a concrete occurrence rather than with an abstract axiom. As Dr. J. G. Machen once remarked, "Christianity is not something that was invented, but something that happened."

The next stage of reasoning carried Paul into the realm of objective theology. "[We] believe on him that raised Jesus our Lord from the dead, who was delivered up for our trespasses, and was raised for our justification" (Rom. 4:24-25).

The doctrine of justification by faith is central to Christian theology. Man, the sinner, possesses no assets by which he can merit or purchase salvation. He stands condemned by his deeds, by his conscience, and by the law, which cannot consistently demand less than perfection of those who attempt to keep it. Even if he desired to obey the law of God, he would not be capable of doing so, for he would be hopelessly handicapped by his past and would be weakened by the habit and presence of sin. In order to attain a satisfactory status with God he must have his record cleared, and he must possess a dynamic empowering him to maintain a holy life.

By the sufferings of Christ these requirements are satisfied. He was "delivered up for our trespasses" (Rom. 4:25), as the final sacrifice sufficient to expiate all human sin. Clearing the charges against man, however, is insufficient, for the sacrifice would not itself guarantee immunity from further sinning. "[He] was raised for our justification" (4:25) in order that He might insure the efficacy of His sacrifice by constant contact with the lives He had redeemed. For this reason Paul adds, "For if, while we were enemies, we were reconciled to God through the death of his Son, much more, being reconciled, shall we be saved by his life" (5:10). The resurrection thus becomes the pledge and dynamic of eternal life.

Baptism, according to Romans, took its meaning from the resurrection rather than from simple purification by washing. "Are ye ignorant that all we who were baptized into Christ Jesus were baptized into his death? We were buried therefore with him through baptism into death: that like as Christ was raised from the dead through the glory of the Father, so we also might walk in newness of life" (6:3-4). From the day of Pentecost (Acts 2:41) to the present, baptism has been the normal method of confessing faith in Christ and of entering the ranks of the visible church. The believer who accepts baptism acknowledges through its symbolism that he has died to sin and has been buried, thereby severing permanently his connection with evil and with the habits and commitments of his former life. Emerging from the engulfing water he enters upon a completely new existence. "Newness of life" (Rom. 6:4), not just redirection, is predicated by this ordinance. The word "newness" (Greek, *kainotēs*) implies freshness, a different kind of life from that which was previously known.

The reality and permanence of the new state are guaranteed by the historical experience of Christ. "For the death that he died, he died unto sin once: but the life that he liveth, he liveth unto God. Even so reckon ye also yourselves to be dead unto sin, but alive unto God in Christ Jesus" (6:10-11). The resurrection is therefore the *basis* of Christian life, not simply the illustration of it. Faith involves not only the acknowledgment of the event but the appropriation of its meaning. The entire concept of sanctification, or progress in the attainment of personal righteousness, is founded upon the assumption that the Christian has been raised out of death and is therefore permanently severed from sin and dedicated to holiness: "present yourselves unto God, as alive from the dead, and your members as instruments of righteousness unto God" (6:13).

Both the ideal and the practical aspects of sanctification are thus linked with Christ's resurrection. The ideal aspect is de-

picted in the historical pattern; the practical aspect emerges from
personal experience. According to the autobiographical data in
Romans, Paul had suffered a serious inner conflict resulting from
his relationship to the law. Like any other devout Jew, he revered
it as the revelation of God's righteousness, and he endeavored
sincerely to keep it. Instead of a sense of security, engendered by
his close approximation of its requirements, he experienced a tor-
menting frustration because his impulses defied his resolutions
and constantly rebelled against his avowed purpose of righteousness. His inner mind became the battlefield of his religious duty
and his personal desires. Far from correcting this condition, the
law could only aggravate the conflict because it increased his
sense of guilt. The more he strove to overcome evil tendencies,
the more powerful they became. "I find then," he said, "that, to
me who would do good, evil is present" (7:21). He was caught
in a deadlock between the ideals that he could not conscientiously
abandon, because he knew that they were the revelation of God,
and the inward trend to evil that he could neither quell nor
eradicate.

The only escape from this dilemma would be the intervention
of an external power to tip the scale one way or the other. Paul
found the solution in Christ, "For the law of the Spirit of life
in Christ Jesus made [him] free from the law of sin and of death"
(8:2). The "law of mind" (7:23), which consented to the law of
God, and "the law of sin," which perpetually led him astray, kept
him in uncertain suspense between good and evil. The "law of
the Spirit" could prevail in favor of righteousness and so assure
victory.

The victory of the Spirit, however, is founded on the resurrection. He is called "the Spirit of him that raised up Jesus from the
dead" (8:11), who expresses in active operation among men the
same kind of power that brought Jesus back to life. True Christianity is, therefore, more than a religion to be adopted; it is a
moral and spiritual dynamic that re-creates the inner life of man
and that transforms his character.

In order to describe adequately the potency of this new life
for the Ephesian Christians, Paul exhausted the resources of his

vocabulary in his prayer. ". . . That ye may know what is . . . the *exceeding greatness* of his *power* to usward who believe, according to that *working* of the *strength* of his *might* which he wrought in Christ, when he raised him from the dead . . ." (Eph. 1:18-20; italics ours).

The italicized words present four aspects of the divine power. "Power" (Gr. *dunamis*) is the latent potential which exists in water restrained behind a dam, or in electric current that can be tapped by turning a switch. When energy is needed to accomplish some task, the means is available. The greatness of God's power is constantly ready for the contact of faith. "Working" (Gr. *energeia*) is applied power, actually operative in a given situation. When latent power is utilized, its effects become visible. "Strength" (Gr. *kratos*) means power in control, as the current flows through the filament of a bulb and masters its elements, making it incandescent. "Might" (Gr. *ischus*) is the result of applied power, conveying to the object controlled a new vigor of its own. These differing concepts have been demonstrated most perfectly in the resurrection of Christ. The latent power was apparent in the force that was sufficient to undo the lethal work of the cross, and to restore Jesus to the fellowship of His disciples. The applied energy opened the grave and renewed His physical life. God's mastery controlled His subsequent activity, enabling Him to appear and vanish at will as He entered upon a new stage of His incarnate existence. This dynamic, perfected in Him and germinal in the believer, is the acknowledged norm of spiritual life.

The correspondence of Christian experience to this pattern was unmistakably declared in the next chapter of Ephesians. "God . . . made us alive . . . with Christ . . . and raised us up with him, and made us to sit with him in the heavenly places, in Christ Jesus" (2:4-6). Paul carried the metaphor one step farther by stressing its result. United with Christ, the believer shares with Him the permanent benefits of His victory. Obviously he has not yet attained the ultimate physical transformation, but he has been transferred to a position of spiritual triumph which provides a new outlook on the world. Resurrection is not merely an isolated

physical event in the life of Christ which provides verification of
His claims; it is also the total spiritual and physical effect produced by the application of the life of God to man's predicament.
The same power that raised Jesus from the dead is inwardly
present and continuous; one day it will be outward and instantaneous. Both aspects constitute salvation by the grace of God.

The fact that Jesus triumphed over death was proof of His
lordship. "Lord" (Gr. *kyrios*) in Graeco-Roman usage was a
common title for a king or emperor. It denoted absolute sovereignty, like the rule of a master over a slave, and also connoted
deity, for it was employed in the worship of the gods. A papyrus
letter of the second century A.D. contains the report of a traveler
who had just concluded a perilous voyage from Rome to Alexandria. He expressed gratitude for his safe arrival by saying, "I
thank the Lord Serapis that when I was in danger on the sea, he
saved me."[1] The title "Lord" gave to Serapis the status of deity.
The same word was generally used by the translators of the
Septuagint to render the Hebrew *Jehovah* and has passed over
into the King James Version of the Bible as LORD. Paul's reason
for ascribing this title to Christ is that He "died, and lived again,
that he might be Lord of both the dead and the living" (Rom.
14:9). The conquest of man's last and most powerful enemy has
confirmed His position as the unique Son of the Father, who
manifests among men the unconquerable life of God.

A further extension of lordship is Christ's right to universal
rulership. He has been exalted to the right hand of God, "far
above all rule, and authority, and power, and dominion, and
every name that is named, not only in this world, but also in that
which is to come" (Eph. 1:21). The seat on the right hand of an
Oriental king was always reserved for his prime minister, who
shared his authority and dignity. Jesus shares with the Father the
sovereign rule over the universe because He has overcome sin and
its accompanying consequence, death.

Paul applied the doctrine of lordship specifically to Christ's

---

[1] George Milligan, *Selections from the Greek Papyri* (Cambridge: University
Press, 1910), pp. 90, 91. Cf. also G. A. Deissmann, *Light from the Ancient East*
(London: Hodder and Stoughton, [1911]), pp. 353-359.

relations with men. Having described the humiliation of Christ through death, he added, "Wherefore also God highly exalted him, and gave unto him the name which is above every name; that in the name of Jesus every knee should bow, of things in heaven and things on earth and things under the earth, and that every tongue should confess that Jesus Christ is Lord, to the glory of God the Father" (Phil. 2:9-11). Because of Christ's exalted position believers are obligated to conduct themselves with humility, since ultimately all men will be compelled to acknowledge His supremacy. Although Paul does not dwell on the exaltation, it is clearly implied in the sudden transition of thought from the humiliation of Christ's death on the cross to the glory of the throne.

The doctrine of the lordship of Christ has far-reaching consequences. It is the deathblow to idolatry, for it extends to Christ the principle of the first commandment, "Thou shalt have no other gods before me" (Exod. 20:3). Paul had been nurtured in the rigidly monotheistic faith of Judaism, and there is no evidence that he ever abandoned it; yet the lordship of Christ did not controvert his concept of the unity and sole majesty of God. "For though there be that are called gods, whether in heaven or on earth; as there are gods many, and lords many; yet to us there is one God, the Father, of whom are all things, and we unto him; and one Lord, Jesus Christ, through whom are all things, and we through him" (I Cor. 8:5-6). Coupled with the name of the Father, the sole source and end of all creation, is the name of Christ, the agent by whom creation came into being and is sustained. By this concept the whole world-view of the Christian was changed. Whereas he had formerly worshiped many gods indiscriminately, he could now bow only at the shrine of Christ. All the common cultic observances that filled the Gentile world were negated at one stroke. "Ye cannot drink the cup of the Lord, and the cup of demons: ye cannot partake of the table of the Lord, and of the table of demons" (I Cor. 10:21). Christianity became an exclusive faith, demanding that its adherents abandon the worship of all other gods.

The exclusiveness of Christ's lordship affected also the Christian's relation to the state. Conflict with government is not reflected strongly in the Pauline Epistles, since the political tension between the Christian Church and the pagan rulers had not become acute during Paul's writing career. The occasional friction with the Roman magistrates whom he encountered in various cities was produced more by local agitation than by any settled imperial policy. Only in the Prison Epistles did he allude to his restraint in chains, and at the close of his life he made a veiled reference to the hostile power of the reigning Caesar when he spoke of being delivered "out of the mouth of the lion" (II Tim. 4:17). The apostle was a loyal citizen of Rome, who urged the Roman Christians to "be in subjection to the higher powers: for . . . the powers that be are ordained of God" (Rom. 13:1). The Christian attitude was not rebellion, but consistent testimony to the lordship of Christ through the manifestation of political integrity.

In event of a clash, however, loyalty to Christ took priority. The Caesars, though mighty, were only men, but Christ was the risen Lord. He became superior to all others and received "the name which is above every name" (Phil. 2:9), to which His followers rendered supreme allegiance and for which they willingly gave their lives under persecution. As Lord "of the living," He possesses the right to take precedence over man's political duties to the state.

Another consequence of Christ's restoration to life is His present ministry of intercession. Having effected a final deliverance from sin by His death, which canceled man's indebtedness to God and established a firm basis for forgiveness, Christ now lives to sustain in holiness those whom He has redeemed. He is able to plead their cause effectively and to defend them against all accusations. "Who is he that condemneth? Shall Christ Jesus who died, yea rather, that was raised from the dead, who is at the right hand of God, who also maketh intercession for us?" (Rom. 8:34, emended translation). The competence of Christ to provide salvation consists both in the completeness of reconciliation to God through the cross and in His contemporary work of nurture and protection.

Although Paul made only a single reference to this doctrine, the context is sufficient to validate it. The Roman church was probably small and weak. Repressive measures under Claudius (A.D. 49), who endeavored to keep Christianity out of the city, had prevented any rapid increase in members. It was largely an underground movement, which had not grown materially during the three years of Nero's reign following the death of Claudius in A.D. 54. The Roman Christians were still insecure and were wondering what new turn the imperial policy might take. Paul mentioned specifically the threatening perils of tribulation, anguish, persecution, famine, nakedness, and the sword (8:35). To encourage these trembling believers, he assured them that nothing could separate them from the love of Christ, but that His intercession for them guaranteed their persistence in faith and their safety. The Christ who has suffered all that man can endure is qualified to ask for all that man needs. He knows how to present their cause to God, and because he has been raised from the dead, He possesses God's pledge that His petitions will be granted.

The fulfillment of God's purpose for Christ's victory over the grave is the key to Pauline eschatology. If Romans is an example of Paul's usual method of presenting Christian truth, he did not elaborate the particulars of the Lord's coming. The eighth chapter of the Epistle contains several hints that the future of the Christians was an integral part of the message and must be included in its total scope. The "firstfruits of the Spirit" (8:23), by which the apostle meant the present operation of the Holy Spirit in daily life, is a precursor of the "redemption of the body," the physical renewal.

Detailed development of this subject appears in Paul's earlier letters to the Corinthians and Thessalonians. The dictum "there is no resurrection of the dead" (I Cor. 15:12), which Paul quoted from his theological adversaries, prompted the argument of the entire fifteenth chapter of I Corinthians. Beginning with the assured fact that Christ has risen, Paul proceeded to treat three corollaries affecting the prospects of the Christian, namely, the program of the future, the nature of the life to come, and the method by which the perfection of redemption would be attained.

The resurrection of Christ was not only a proof that the dead can be raised but a promise that they would be raised. Christ was the first to demonstrate the redemptive exercise of divine power that reverses the trend beginning with the disobedience of Adam. The cumulative effects of sin have made death, both spiritual and physical, the supreme tragedy of the race. For redemption to be effective, the hope of resurrection must be extended to all mankind who are in Christ since God's program for the future requires this objective. The emergence of Christ from death is the beginning; next in order will be the raising of those to whom He has imparted life; and finally will come the perfection of the kingdom which will be the outward demonstration of the authority of Christ over Satan, and of life over death.

Neither the fine details of this program nor the dates for its fulfillment are supplied by Scripture, nor are they important. The main aspect of Paul's argument is that God has introduced a new dynamic into the course of human existence, capable of transforming it from a purposeless round of failure into a progressive march toward triumph. Through this decisive act God has revealed His intended destiny for man. Like a light in darkness it offers direction for bewildered travelers, although it may not yet have dispelled all the shadows.

The nature of the future hope is exemplified in Christ's permanent release from the bonds of humanity. "Christ being raised from the dead dieth no more; death no more hath dominion over him" (Rom. 6:9). The liberty of the gospel extends to freedom from the enslavement of sin and from the fear and hopelessness of death, for "the creation itself also shall be delivered from the bondage of corruption into the liberty of the glory of the children of God" (8:21). Just as Christ left the humiliation of death and the corruption of the grave to resume His place in the glory of the Father's presence, the believers in Him will share His experience.

Perfection will be attained when He returns to complete the work of salvation. The reign of death will be terminated by the appearance of Christ. "We all shall not sleep, but we shall all be changed . . . for the trumpet shall sound, and the dead shall be raised incorruptible, and we shall be changed. . . . But when this corruptible shall have put on incorruption, and this mortal shall have put on immortality, then shall come to pass the saying that is written, Death is swallowed up in victory" (I Cor. 15:51-54). The translation from imperfection to completeness and from mortality to immortality will be instantaneous and will commence the eternal state which is the goal and fulfillment of salvation.

The final concept of the resurrection in Pauline preaching is its evangelistic appeal. Repeatedly in his Epistles Paul summons his readers to profess faith in Christ. The profession must necessarily be simple, for few believers begin their Christian life with an elaborate creed, and yet it must be inclusive enough to insure a complete foundation for faith. Confession of Christ's lordship is contingent on acceptance of the fact of the resurrection and on the experience of the life of God in Christ exhibited in His triumph over death. "If thou shalt confess with thy mouth Jesus as Lord, and shalt believe in thy heart that God raised him from the dead, thou shalt be saved: for with the heart man believeth unto righteousness; and with the mouth confession is made unto salvation" (Rom. 10:9-10). It is a leap from the visible to the invisible, from evidence to promise, and from pessimism to hope.

When at the close of his life Paul was about to relinquish his position of missionary leadership, he was concerned that the theme of the gospel might continue to be proclaimed with undiminished fervor. Some teachers had appeared who maintained that "the resurrection is past already" (II Tim. 2:18). In farewell instructions to his understudy, Timothy, Paul included numerous directions for church administration, but the central message was "Remember Jesus Christ, risen from the dead, of the seed of David, according to my gospel" (II Tim. 2:8).

The Pauline teaching shows that an articulated theology based on Jesus' return from death had been accepted in the church before the end of the first century. Springing from the principle of life in Christ, and demonstrated in the personal life of the apostle, it became the core of Christian doctrine and the motive of its evangelistic mission.

The Petrine Epistles

The genuineness of I and II Peter has been disputed and frequently denied, but the negative evidence is not strong enough
to warrant excluding them from consideration. Both claim to
have been written by Peter himself or with the aid of an aman-
uensis, and both professedly reflect his life and teaching. Although Peter occupied a less prominent place in the New
Testament than Paul, he was important, for his priority in time
compensates for the paucity of his literary contributions. According to Luke's account of the early church (Acts 15:6-21), both
attended the Council of Jerusalem, probably A.D. 48, and both
defended Gentile freedom of conscience against the Judaizing
party that insisted on circumcision. After the council Peter vanished from the narrative, while Paul began his second missionary
journey and became the protagonist of the gospel along the
northern shores of the Mediterranean Sea from Antioch to Asia
Minor.

Insofar as the effects of Peter's preaching are traceable, they
indicate a high concept of the importance of the resurrection.
Both Peter and Paul were eyewitnesses of the risen Christ (I Cor.
15:5, 8), and both made the doctrine prominent in their ministry.
Of the two, however, Peter was more pragmatic in his apologetic
and evangelistic approach, while Paul was more speculative. The
speeches and writings attributed to Peter say little about the nature of the resurrection body, or about the theological significance
of the victory over death.

For Peter Jesus' reappearance was primarily the vindication of
a cause. Perhaps this difference of emphasis resulted from personal experience. Having expected that Jesus would establish a
visible kingdom in which he might hold office, and having suffered the disappointment and frustration occasioned by the crucifixion, Peter was tempted to abandon the entire enterprise as
hopeless. The Master's return confirmed His promises, so in-
adequately understood by the disciples, and revitalized the positive teaching apparently vitiated by His death. Peter regained
courage and undertook to follow Christ with new zeal and devo-

tion when he realized that his Lord was alive.

Peter's approach is more personal than that of Paul, perhaps because he had more ample opportunity to maintain contact with Jesus in His human relationships. Before Paul's conversion, Jesus was to him a public figure known only by reputation, but Peter had claimed Jesus as a close friend. Paul initially regarded the death of Christ as the salutary removal of a dangerous heretic; Peter had mourned His loss as a personal tragedy. His sudden transition from despair to delight is reflected in the opening words of his letter, "Blessed be the God and Father of our Lord Jesus Christ, who according to his great mercy begat us again unto a living hope by the resurrection of Jesus Christ from the dead . . ." (I Pet. 1:3). So revolutionary was this experience that Peter calls it a new birth, effected by "the word of God, which liveth and abideth" (1:23). In contrast to the transiency of the flesh, which withers like grass, the new life remains permanently.

Without minimizing the literal, historical, and eschatological aspects of the resurrection, Peter stressed its moral effect. Hope was the watchword of the new faith, contrasting sharply with his preceding pessimism. He opposed a cynical skepticism with a positive optimism based on the reality of God, who had intervened in his experience and who could transform the lives of others also.

The trust in a sovereign God was grounded in the historic fact. "Through him [Christ, ye] are believers in God, that raised him from the dead, and gave him glory; so that your faith and hope might be in God" (1:21). Peter's words parallel Paul's in Galatians 1:1 both in literal statement and in the implication that the essential character of God is defined by His vivifying act. Life is God's nature; it is irrepressible, and He cannot exist without acting creatively. The supreme manifestation of this life is both the object and the incentive of faith.

Another facet is its mystical relation to the believer's position in Christ. In a rather obscure passage in the third chapter of his first epistle, Peter speaks of baptism as ". . . the interrogation [marginal reading: inquiry] of a good conscience toward God, through the resurrection of Jesus Christ; who is on the right hand of God, having gone into heaven; angels and authorities and powers being made subject unto him" (3:21-22). Peter, like Paul, connected the symbolism with the resurrection of Christ. His teaching was analogous to Paul's, but not identical, for he did not place the same emphasis on the concept of union with Christ (cf. Rom. 6:2-11). Having affirmed that Christ died to take away sins (I Pet. 3:18), he explained baptism as the response to God by the newly imparted life. The sequence of the following verses confirms this interpretation: "that ye no longer should live the rest of your time in the flesh to the lusts of men, but to the will of God" (4:2). The trammels of sin have been released, and a different sphere of liberty has been opened.

No definite teaching is contained in II Peter, but the allusion to Paul's Epistles (II Pet. 3:15, 16) makes more plausible a connection of thought between Peter and Paul. Although Peter did not copy the Pauline application, his language shows an underlying agreement with it. Both accepted the historic fact, and both used it as a pattern for the personal experience of the believer.

The Epistle to the Hebrews

Parallel to the Pauline and Petrine Epistles, the book of Hebrews contains a statement of Christian faith that was designed for broad application although addressed to a specific constituency. The exact identity of that group is one of the thorniest problems in New Testament scholarship, and its solution is debatable. Hebrews was written by a man well versed in the Greek Septuagint. The recipients, Jewish by ancestry and Christian by conviction, were facing the dilemma of renouncing their Christian faith for the sake of placating their relatives, or of continuing with Christ and suffering consequent persecution. Among the numerous Jewish Christian churches in the first century, the one addressed in this Epistle cannot be located with certainty. A plausible case can be constructed for identifying it with the church in Rome about A.D. 68. At that time the persecution under Nero had ceased, but its renewal was always an imminent threat, and the memory of harassment and official pressure was still vivid (Heb. 10:32-34).

Whatever the local destination may have been, Hebrews was addressed to second-generation Christians who had not seen the Lord, but who were familiar with His teaching and who worshiped Him (2:3). The Epistle marked an interim stage in the development of the church between the disciplinary letters of Paul, directed largely to new churches, and the more contemplative Johannine writings designed for a settled institutional body.

The chief theme of Hebrews is the intercessory priestly ministry of Christ (8:3, 4), mentioned by Paul in Romans but developed more fully to counteract the discouraging effects of persecution. The entire treatise assumes the resurrection of Christ and contains several unmistakable references to the doctrine. Unlike Paul, the author does not attempt an apologetic defense of the fact; he simply takes it for granted, dealing with the results rather than with the event itself.

The initial statement declares the Christology on which its entire argument is built. The Son, having revealed to men the glory of the Father and having removed sin by His incarnate ministry, has now "sat down on the right hand of the Majesty on high" (1:3). While the exaltation of Christ to the Father's throne should not be interpreted as a spiritualization of the physical fact, the two events were inseparably linked in the mind of the writer, who interpreted the cause in terms of the effect. The deliverance from death was axiomatic and undebatable; the result in the intercessory ministry was the application that he wished to develop.

The session of Christ on the right hand of God was, therefore, the guarantee of His effective contemporary ministry. Since He had passed through death He could understand the plight of those who are doomed to death, and could, by the exercise of the same power that restored Him to life, liberate them from fear of death (2:14, 15). The entire doctrine of the priesthood of Christ, involving His representation of the people of God and His perpetual service to them, is founded on the unending life that enables Him to maintain His office without interruption. "Wherefore also he is able to save to the uttermost them that draw near unto God through him, seeing he ever liveth to make intercession for them" (7:25).

The concept of resurrection was no novelty either to the author of Hebrews or to his readers, for it was enumerated among the basic teachings bequeathed to them from Judaism. "Resurrection of the dead" and "eternal judgment" were among the "first principles" of Messianic doctrine. "Leaving" these principles (6:1) did not denote repudiation, but rather a progress to the realization of the truths growing out of them. The Old Testament and the Apocrypha contained allusions to the doctrine, but the practical understanding of its significance came only through the work of Christ. For this reason the writer of Hebrews urged his readers to "press on unto perfection" (6:1).

The dual application of deliverance from fear (2:14, 15) and the pledge of Christ's unfailing intercessory ministry (7:25) had special value for a persecuted church. Since they were constantly haunted by the grim specter of death, they craved victory over fear and over the sense of futility that such a threat entailed. For that reason the doctrine of the resurrection was incorporated in the famous "faith chapter" (chap. 11). In reviewing various examples of faith, the writer recalled Abraham's readiness to sacrifice Isaac and remarked that the patriarch believed in God's power to raise the dead. Had Isaac actually died, all of God's promises and Abraham's hopes would have perished; if Abraham did not obey God's command, his disobedience would preclude further divine revelation or favor. While Abraham probably did not have a well-defined concept of God's intention, he had unlimited confidence in the ability of God to validate His promise. His faith was justified in the restoration of Isaac, which was a picture of a greater reality.

In the same chapter there is a second allusion to martyrs, probably Maccabeans, who refused deliverance "that they might obtain a better resurrection" (11:35). The writer conceived of it not simply as the inevitable consummation of a saving process uni-

formly applied to all believers but as a reward for faithfulness.
Status in the resurrection might be attained by self-sacrifice. The
writer did not define his meaning, but he spoke of God's provision of "some better thing" (11:40), or of the joy set before
Christ at the right hand of God (12:2), or of "the city of the
living God, the heavenly Jerusalem" (12:22).

The closing benediction of the Epistle incorporates words
which may have been taken from the form customarily recited at
the close of a worship service. "Now the God of peace, who
brought again from the dead the great shepherd of the sheep
with the blood of an eternal covenant, even our Lord Jesus, make
you perfect in every good thing to do his will . . ." (13:20-21).
The import of the prayer is unmistakable. The assurance of
preservation and of perfection promised to the persecuted
Hebrew Christians was founded on the shepherd character of
Christ revealed in the resurrection. It recalls the words of Jesus,
"I am the good shepherd . . . and I lay down my life for the
sheep. . . . No one taketh it away from me, but I lay it down of
myself. I have power to lay it down, and I have power to take it
again" (John 10:14, 15, 18). In the catacombs of Rome which
sheltered the refugee church of the second and third centuries,
one of the most common representations of Christ is the Good
Shepherd, with a lamb on His shoulders. The use of this symbol
reflected confidence in the protecting power of the Saviour, who
had given His life for the salvation of His people and who rose
again to guard them from their enemies. Even though they should
pass through the valley of the shadow of death He would be able
to conduct them to the Father's house.

Hebrews marks a new stage in the development of the doctrine. Whereas the speeches of Acts stress the basic fact that "God
raised him from the dead," this Epistle takes for granted the historical and apologetic aspect and applies the wider ramifications
of the principle. The resurrection of Christ is the foundation of
His present intercession, the source of freedom from fear of
death, and the assurance of His continued guardianship through
persecution.

The Johannine Writings

The Johannine Epistles and Revelation were the last canonical writings of the apostolic age, written within the decade between A.D. 85 and 95. The Fourth Gospel, though discussed previously in conjunction with the Synoptics, is a part of this body of literature and should be classed with it. The traditional authorship of Revelation, on the other hand, has been challenged by many scholars, who cannot reconcile its style and language with that of the Gospel and Epistles. While circumstances and subject matter may be sufficient to account for the disparity, the question of authorship need not disturb seriously the testimony of Revelation. A product of the first century, it reproduces accurately the spiritual climate of the closing years.

The Epistles contain no specific argument for the resurrection, nor does the word itself occur in them; nevertheless they bear traces of its influence. The opening words of I John, which parallel those of the Gospel, summarize it in terms of life. "That which was from the beginning, that which we have heard, that which we have seen with our eyes, that which we beheld, and our hands handled, concerning the Word of life (and the life was manifested, and we have seen, and bear witness, and declare unto you the life, the eternal *life*, which was with the Father, and was manifested unto us) . . ." (I John 1:1-2).

The repetitiousness of these introductory verses emphasizes the material manifestation of eternal life, for it was not an abstract ideal but was visible, tangible, and audible. "Life," which occurs three times in the Greek text of the first two verses, is the opposite of death and expresses the essence of the revelation in Christ which the author proceeds to expound, and to apply to his readers. On the assumption that the First Epistle is a sequel to the Gospel of John, the principle of "life" is built on the presupposition that Christ is the resurrection and the life, and that subsequent to His death, to which the Epistle alludes (1:7, 4:10, 5:6), He arose to confirm His promise (5:11).

The parallel between the language of the introduction to I John and the resurrection narrative in the Gospel of John is obvious. The verb *see* (Gr. *heōrakamen*) appears in the testimony of the disciples to Thomas (John 20:25). Thomas *heard* the voice of Jesus speaking to him and was given the opportunity to *handle* His body (20:27), whether he actually did so or not. The others likewise saw Him, heard Him, and touched Him. The doctrine of eternal life is a logical consequence of Jesus' demonstration that His vitality could not be extinguished, but that His power could transcend death.

The broad scope of the eternal life manifested in Christ is unfolded. His present intercessory ministry mentioned by Paul (Rom. 8:34) and expanded in Hebrews (7:25 ff.) is included also in John's message. He calls Christ the "Advocate" who perpetually pleads His people's cause on the basis of His propitiatory sacrifice (I John 2:1, 2). The promise "he that doeth the will of God abideth for ever" (2:17) recalls the word of the Saviour, who said, "I seek not mine own will, but the will of him that sent me" (John 5:30), and proved later by rising from the tomb that He would "abide for ever." The future transformation of the children of God at the Lord's appearing will be the open and visible proclamation of their sonship, as the resurrection declared Him to be the Son of God with power (Rom. 1:4). The exhortation to love one another (I John 4:7 ff.) is an echo of Jesus' post-resurrection challenge to Peter, "Lovest thou me?" (John 22:15-17). The overcoming of the world (I John 5:4, 5) is patterned on Jesus' triumph after death had done its worst (John 16:28, 33).

Revelation, the last book in the order of the New Testament canon and in time of writing, constitutes the bridge between the age of the apostles and the rise of the institutional church. Written to seven churches of Asia during the reign of Domitian (A.D. 81-96), it depicted the emerging consciousness of antagonism between the gospel and paganism, between Christ and the Caesars. The repressive measures that later developed into wholesale persecution had already begun, although the hostility between Rome and the churches was not yet so acute as it became in the second century. Attacks upon Christians were sporadic, and persecution was probably more an evidence of local prejudice than a settled governmental policy. Nevertheless, the battle line was plainly drawn, and the Christians realized that they were involved in an irrepressible conflict. Since the pressure was increasing, they were concerned lest their movement fail.

The visions of the Apocalypse were granted to the seer to prepare the churches for the impending struggle. By addressing seven representative communities, the divine author conveyed to the entire church His message concerning its weaknesses, perils, and destiny. The Apocalypse is prophecy cast in pictorial form so that the discerning Christian reader may understand its predictions, while the hostile pagan will dismiss it as a harmless dream. Although the details of its symbolism may not always be clear to the modern student, he can comprehend the main principles that it illustrates.

The opening paragraph of Revelation provides the key to the book by presenting the person of Christ, calling Him "the firstborn of the dead" (Rev. 1:5). "Firstborn" implies priority both in time and in position. He is the first of many who will rise from death and is consequently the originator and head of the eternal community of God's people. Having overcome death, He is able to cope with the destructive powers of evil and to abolish their dominion forever. As the drama of the Apocalypse progresses to its consummation in the City of God, the intervention of the risen Christ is apparent at every stage.

To the church at Smyrna the seer wrote: "These things saith the first and the last, who was dead, and lived again . . . [or, *came to life*]" (2:8). He reiterated the self-identification of Christ in His initial appearance, "I was dead, and behold, I am alive for evermore, and I have the keys of death and of Hades" (1:18). This greeting to a suffering and persecuted church was particularly appropriate, for it offered the assurance that Christ had passed through the same conflict and that He had emerged triumphant. During the present age the church militant rests its hope in a living Lord who is already victorious over death.

The predictive section depicting the scene in heaven (4:1-16:21) centers its interest on the Lamb which had been slain (5:6). He bore the marks of death and yet was alive. By the return to life the Lamb prevailed "to open the book and the seven seals thereof" (5:5). He had earned the prerogative of introducing the judgments that clear corruption from the earth, and that prepare the way for the eternal kingdom.

In the exercise of this power the resurrection becomes the basis of His sovereignty. The action of Revelation is an extended exposition of the prophecy in Psalm 2.

I will tell of the decree:
Jehovah said unto me, Thou art my son;
This day have I begotten thee.
Ask of me, and I will give thee the nations for thine inheritance,
And the uttermost parts of the earth for thy possession.
Thou shalt break them with a rod of iron;
Thou shalt dash them in pieces like a potter's vessel (Ps. 2:7-9).

The sequence of the predicted events indicates that Messiah's rulership over the nations is founded upon His right of sonship. Paul, in his address to the synagogue at Antioch of Pisidia, declared the Psalm to be prophetic. "God hath . . . raised up Jesus; as also it is written in the second psalm, Thou art my Son, this day have I begotten thee" (Acts 13:33). If the judgments of Revelation are the result of Christ's exercise of His prerogatives of sonship, then the eschatology of this book is the outcome and conclusion of His unprecedented triumph over death.

Two aspects of resurrection are connected with the establishment of the millennial kingdom. One concerns the souls of the righteous that "lived, and reigned with Christ a thousand years" (Rev. 20:4). The verb *lived* can equally well be rendered "came to life," implying a sudden event rather than a process. Since the subject is "those who had been beheaded," the verb cannot mean "they had lived and reigned," for their death occurred before the thousand years began. The sentence refers to the future and demands a restoration of the righteous dead who will share in the rule of Christ.

The second aspect relates to "the rest of the dead [who] lived not [did not come to life] until the thousand years should be finished" (20:5). Since the resurrection of the second group is manifestly an event, and not a process, a correct analogy demands that the resurrection of the first group also be an event. The righteous, then, will be summoned back to life in order that they may reign with Christ; the wicked, "the rest of the dead," will be haled to judgment. When they shall have been judged and their final status fixed, death itself will be destroyed (20:13, 14). That which the resurrection of Christ began the resurrection of men will conclude.

The vision of the city of God (21:9-22:5), from which all evil is permanently excluded, previews the consummation. The "tree of life," the leaves of which are for the healing of the nations (22:2), is emblematic of the inexhaustible source of spiritual and physical vitality available in the age to come. The climax of the Apocalypse demonstrates that the manifestation of life which began in Joseph's garden will attain its full glory in the paradise of God.

V *An Emergent Creed*

The close of the first century introduced a critical stage in the life of the Christian church. The death of the apostles removed any possibility of adding firsthand testimony to the record of teaching that had constituted the gospel message, and the pioneering assemblies began to assume the organizational form foreshadowed in the Pastoral and Johannine Epistles. Beginning as a sect of Judaism, and developing as an independent movement that received increasing support from Gentiles, Christianity finally emerged at the end of the second century as a world religion and as a potent social factor in the Roman empire. During the time of missionary expansion under Paul in the reigns of Claudius and Nero (A.D. 41-68) the church had been largely underground. Its adherents were either Jews, who were protected by law, or a low class of Gentiles whose cult was patronizingly considered to be irrational but harmless. The Neronian persecution, being confined to Rome, was local in scope and was the result of a desire to find a scapegoat for the burning of the city, rather than of a studied attempt to exterminate a religious minority. The reputed persecution under Domitian was a reaction to the Christians' refusal to worship the emperor as Lord and God, for the Roman public objected to their practice rather than to their theory. Not until the Antonine emperors (A.D. 170) was Christianity openly declared inimical to the state and persecuted because of its inherent character.

By the end of the second century the infant church had grown to a powerful minority. Tertullian (A.D. 200) was able to boast, "There is no nation indeed which is not Christian."[1] "We are but of yesterday," he said, "and we have filled every place among you —cities, islands, fortresses, towns, market-places, the very camp, tribes, companies, palace, senate, forum—we have left nothing to you but the temples of your gods."[2]

Despite some rhetorical exaggeration, Tertullian's claim was undoubtedly substantiated by the facts. The empire would not have been alarmed by a feeble and insignificant sect, but when a large proportion of the population became Christian, and when the protagonists of the new message proved to be keen debaters and persuasive preachers, the pagan world feared revolution. Christian belief and Christian ethics had made serious inroads into the old religions of the gods and had changed drastically many of the social customs.

The process by which this development took place is not well known, for the Christians were not voluminous writers, and they paid scant attention to recording their own accomplishments. War, persecution, and the inevitable decay of time have left few vestiges of the literature of this period, so that the progress of Christianity in the second century can be traced only imperfectly. It is, however, amply certain that the resurrection was an essential element in Christian theology and a leading topic in apologetic preaching.

The earliest noncanonical writing surviving from the sub-apostolic age is the *Epistle of Clement,* written from Rome to the church of Corinth about A.D. 95. The writer was attempting to correct certain abuses which had entered the Corinthian church, and he appealed to the purity of the apostolic message for his authority. "The apostles have preached the gospel to us from the Lord Jesus Christ; Jesus Christ [has done so] from God. Christ therefore was sent forth by God, and the apostles by

[1] Tertullian, *Ad Nationes* VIII.
[2] Tertullian, *Apologia* XXXVIII.

Christ. . . . Having therefore received their orders, and being
fully assured by the resurrection of our Lord Jesus Christ . . .
they went forth proclaiming that the kingdom of God was at
hand."[3] According to Clement, the resurrection was the foundation and confirmation of the apostolic commission and message.
He proclaimed it as an unquestioned verity accepted by the
apostles and their successors.

The historical fact is also the pledge of hope for the future,
since it guarantees that believers will be raised from death.

Let us consider, beloved, how the Lord continually proves to
us that there shall be a future resurrection, of which he has
rendered the Lord Jesus Christ the first-fruits by raising him from
the dead. Let us contemplate, beloved, the resurrection which is
at all times taking place. Day and night declare to us a resurrection. The night sinks to sleep, and the day arises; the day [again]
departs, and the night comes on. Let us behold the fruits [of the
earth], how the sowing of grain takes place. . . the seed being
. . . scattered, though dry and naked when it fell upon the earth,
is gradually dissolved. Then out of its dissolution the mighty
power of the providence of the Lord raises it up again, and from
one seed many arise and bring forth fruit.[4]

Clement cited as another illustration the example of the
phoenix, a fabled Arabian bird, which reputedly died and was
reborn every five hundred years.

Let us consider that wonderful sign [of the resurrection] which
takes place in Eastern lands, that is, in Arabia and the countries
round about. There is a certain bird which is called a phoenix.
This is the only one of its kind, and lives five hundred years.
And when the time of its dissolution draws near that it must die,
it builds itself a nest of frankincense, and myrrh, and other spices,
into which, when the time is fulfilled, it enters and dies. But as
the flesh decays a certain kind of worm is produced, which, being
nourished by the juices of the dead bird, brings forth feathers.
Then, when it has acquired strength, it takes up that nest in
which are the bones of its parent, and bearing these it passes
from the land of Arabia into Egypt, to the city called Heliopolis.
And, in open day, flying in the sight of all men, it places them on

---

[3] *I Clement* XLII.
[4] *Ibid.*, XXIV.

the altar of the sun, and having done this, hastens back to its former abode. The priests then inspect the registers of the dates, and find that it has returned exactly as the five hundredth year was completed.[5]

Clement's method of argument was necessarily that of his own time and was consequently quite unscientific, but his convictions imply a firm belief in the physical resurrection of Christ. He followed the fable of the phoenix by an appeal to the Scriptures, quoting Psalms 28:7 and 3:6 and Job 19:25, 26. The first quotation is so loose that the reference is only probable; the second and third are unmistakable.[6] Clement undoubtedly believed that the words of the Old Testament foreshadowed Christ's personal victory over death, and that they should be applied literally.

In the first decade of the second century, immediately following Clement, Ignatius of Antioch wrote a short series of letters to individual friends and churches. Fifteen in all have been attributed to him, but only seven are acknowledged to be genuine: the epistles to the Ephesians, to the Magnesians, to the Trallians, to the Romans, to the Philadelphians, to the Smyrneans, and to Polycarp. The first three exist only in Latin; the rest are known also in Greek. There are two editions of the seven letters, one shorter and one longer. It is generally agreed that the longer edition was amplified by later editors, and that the shorter edition is the one that Ignatius actually wrote.[7]

The correspondence of Ignatius affords a fair index of the teaching at 'Antioch in the closing years of the first century and the beginning of the second century when he resided there. Sixty years had passed since that church had been founded during Paul's initial ministry to the Gentiles. The leadership

---

[5] *Ibid.*, XXV.

[6] *Ibid.*, XXVI. Compare also Ch. XLII where Clement asserts that the resurrection is a confirmation of apostolic authority.

[7] See R. Travers Smith, "St. Ignatius," in *Dictionary of Christian Biography*, William Smith and Henry Wace, editors (London: John Murray, 1882), III, 210a, 212a, b; G. Uhlhorn, "Ignatius of Antioch," in *The New Schaff-Herzog Encyclopedia of Religious Knowledge* (New York and London: Funk & Wagnalls, 1909), V, 445, 446, See also R. M. Grant, "Ignatius of Antioch," in *Twentieth Century Encyclopedia of Religious Knowledge*, Lefferts A. Loetscher, editor (Grand Rapids, Mich.: Baker Book House, 1935), I, 546, 547.

of Antioch had increasingly become a superintendence over other churches, and Ignatius, the senior pastor, was attempting to fortify his fellow Christians elsewhere against the impending persecution of Trajan (A.D. 110-117), in which he himself died a martyr at Rome. His writing and preaching illustrate the doctrinal growth of the church as it began to resist the moral and philosophical pressures of the pagan world.

In his opening letter to the church at Smyrna Ignatius defined his creed. Christ ". . . was truly born of a virgin, was baptized by John, in order that all righteousness might be fulfilled by Him; and was truly, under Pontius Pilate and Herod the tetrarch, nailed [to the cross] for us in His flesh. Of this fruit we are by His divinely-blessed passion, that He might set up a standard for all ages, through His resurrection, to all His holy and faithful [followers], whether among Jews or Gentiles, in the one body of His Church."[8] Because of persecution, Ignatius was especially desirous of promoting unity. The creed afforded a platform for a united faith; the resurrection was the power that produced a unity of spirit.

In contrast to the Docetists, who held that Christ was only an apparition, Ignatius insisted on physical reality. He disposed of the "apparition" or "vision" theory by saying, "He truly raised up himself, not, as certain unbelievers maintain, that he only appeared to suffer. . . ."[9] After the resurrection, Jesus still existed in flesh, and Ignatius alluded to the scriptural affirmations that Jesus could be touched and could eat.[10] In a reference to the Lord's Supper he spoke of "the flesh of our Saviour Jesus Christ, which suffered for our sins, and which the Father . . . raised."[11]

The Epistle to the Trallians contained another creedal statement quite similar to that in the Epistle to the Smyrneans. Ignatius linked the resurrection of Christ definitely with that of the believer. "And truly he was raised from the dead, since his Father raised him. In similar fashion the Father will raise up us who

---

8 *Smyrneans* I.
9 *Ibid.*, II.
10 *Ibid.*, III.
11 *Ibid.*, VII.

believe in him, by Christ Jesus, apart from whom we have no real life."[12]

Writing to the Philadelphians, Ignatius argued with those who refused to believe the gospel unless it were substantiated by the ancient Scriptures. "As far as I am concerned," he replied, "Jesus Christ stands for the ancient things: His cross, His death, His resurrection, and the faith which comes through Him are the sacred heritage of antiquity."[13] "The Gospel possesses a certain distinctive feature, the appearance of the Saviour, the Lord Jesus Christ, His sufferings and His death. For the beloved prophets proclaimed Him, but the gospel is the completion of immortality."[14]

The objection which Ignatius' opponents had raised sprang from Judaism, and possibly from the Sadducean tradition. Because the resurrection had not been predicted in detail, they refused to accept it. Ignatius contended that the life of Christ was self-authenticating. He did not deny that predictions might be found in the Scriptures, or that they contained truth, but he was insisting upon the authority of the gospel as the product of God's revelation in Christ.

Ignatius' use of the word "gospel" is slightly ambiguous. Did he mean the general content of the Christian revelation, or was he referring to the narrative tradition of the life of Christ? In either case the resurrection was one of the distinguishing marks of the new message that differentiated it from all other cults and teaching of his time and formed the basis for the development of Christian theology.

The cardinal truths which he stressed in these three epistles were reiterated in the letter to the Magnesians. "These things, my beloved, [I write unto you] not because I know that any of you are in such an error [Judaizing], but because I want the very least of you to guard yourselves lest you be caught like a fish on the hooks of false doctrine, and that you may have full assurance regarding the birth and suffering and the resurrection which oc-

---

[12] *Trallians* IX.
[13] *Philadelphians* VIII.
[14] *Ibid.,* IX.

curred in the time of the governorship of Pontius Pilate. . . ."[15] The repeated identification of doctrine with historical fact substantiates the principle that the church's faith was built on the person of Christ rather than upon speculation.

Polycarp, a younger contemporary of the apostles and an associate of Ignatius, who died a martyr in A.D. 155, wrote an epistle to the Philippian church. In alluding to some of his predecessors, like Ignatius, he said, "For they did not 'love this present world' but him who died on our behalf, and was raised by God for our sakes."[16] The hope of personal resurrection appeared also in his writing, for he said, "He has promised that he will raise us again from the dead . . . provided only we believe."[17]

A somewhat different application appears in the *Epistle of Barnabas,* dated in the first half of the second century[18] and written as an apologetic against Judaism. Explaining Jesus' relation to prophecy, the author declared that the resurrection was a necessary factor in salvation. "And He (since it behoved Him to appear in flesh), that He might abolish death and reveal the resurrection from the dead, endured [what and as He did], in order that He might fulfill the promise made unto the fathers, and by preparing a new people for Himself, might show, while He dwelt on earth, that He, when He has raised mankind, will also judge them."[19]

The testimony of this author connects the victory of Christ over death with present and future salvation. Ignatius had said that the gospel was final authority,[20] but the *Epistle of Barnabas* extended the principle by accepting the resurrection as a necessary part of Christ's incarnation and as a pledge of future judgment. The discussion is not detailed, but its implications are

---

[15] *Magnesians* XI.

[16] Polycarp, *To the Philippians* IX, 2.

[17] *Ibid.,* V, 1.

[18] K. Lake, *Apostolic Fathers* (London: Heinemann, 1919), 339, says: "The document no doubt belongs to the end of the first or beginning of the second century." It was treated as canonical by some churches, being included among the New Testament books in Codex Aleph, with no indication that it belonged to a secondary classification.

[19] *Epistle of Barnabas* V.

[20] See fn. 14.

broad, and afford latitude for further expansion.

The first extant treatise on the general doctrine was written by Justin Martyr, a Syrian Greek philosopher, about A.D. 150. He was familiar with many of the objections that are still current today, and he attempted to answer them. His chief argument against his opponents was the resurrection of Christ.

> If the resurrection was only spiritual it was requisite that he, in raising the dead, should show the body lying apart by itself and the soul living apart by itself. . . . Why did he rise in the flesh in which he suffered, unless to show the resurrection of the flesh? And wishing to confirm this, when his disciples did not know whether to believe he had truly risen in the body and were looking upon him and doubting, he said to them, "Ye have not yet faith, see that it is I;" and he let them handle him and showed them the print of the nails in his hands.[21]

By "spiritual resurrection" Justin referred to the concept held by many Greek thinkers that there would be no reconstitution of the flesh. They were quite modern in their contention that Jesus Himself appeared only in a subjective vision, and not in tangible bodily form.

In his *Apology*[22] Justin had contended for the renewal of the material body, arguing that the natural development of bones and sinews from a small drop of semen is not more likely than the reconstitution of that same structure in the resurrection. Although the argument from comparative probability may not seem cogent because concepts of the constitution and presentation of matter have changed, his method of reasoning introduced a new approach to the material world. He anticipated the scientific method by recognizing the importance of the material world without surrendering to materialism. At the same time he stressed the spiritual significance of the resurrection without making it illusory or subjective by depriving it of historical reality. Justin discovered the starting point for a new Christian realism.

During the last third of the second century, between the per-

---

[21] Justin Martyr, *Fragments of the Lost Work on the Resurrection* IX.
[22] Justin Martyr, *Apology* I, xix.

secutions under Marcus Aurelius (A.D. 177) and Severus (A.D. 202),
Christianity was confronted with the danger of Gnosticism, a
fusion of Oriental mysticism and Greek idealism which invaded
the Christian community and threatened to pervert its theology.
There was a consequent increase in the polemic literature of the
church, whose leaders undertook to combat the insidious heresy.
Chief among the writers was Irenaeus, Bishop of Lyons in France
from A.D. 177 to 190, whose major work, *Against Heresies,* in five
volumes, is the primary source for knowledge of his teaching.

Irenaeus wrestled with the same problems that had vexed
Justin Martyr: the nature of the resurrection body and the
method of its reconstruction from the decayed remnants of the
present body. His chief attack, however, was directed toward
the Gnostic contention that since the body was inherently corrupt
and was not worth preserving, a bodily resurrection not only
would be an impossibility but would be undesirable. In his
counterarguments Irenaeus followed generally the same procedure as Justin Martyr, except that he made much fuller use
of the New Testament.[23]

Irenaeus reasoned that since it must be more difficult to create
man out of nothing than to reintegrate the material that has
decomposed, the resurrection is less incredible than the original
creation. If God made man's flesh capable of life, He can re-
create it capable of eternal life. There is no inherent impossibility
in resurrection; it depends on the creative power of God, who
has already demonstrated that power by raising Christ from the
dead. If the flesh was capable of corruption, it was also capable
of incorruption. Corruptible life was imparted by the breath of
God; incorruptible life, by the Spirit of God.[24] The breath is
transient; the spirit is eternal.

In contrast to the Gnostic theory that the material body is
too gross and carnal to become the vehicle of eternal life, Irenaeus
argued that the raising of Jairus' daughter, the young man at
Cana, and Lazarus prefigured the final resurrection. He insisted
on the identity of the body interred with the body resurrected.

[23] Irenaeus, *Against Heresies* V, iii, 2.
[24] *Ibid.,* V, xii, 1, 2.

"What then is this 'body of humiliation' which the Lord shall transfigure, [making it] conformed to 'the body of his glory'? Plainly it is the body composed of flesh, which is indeed humbled when it falls into the earth. Now its transformation [takes place there], that while it is mortal and corruptible, it becomes immortal and incorruptible . . . after the mighty working of the Lord, who is able to invest the mortal with immortality and the corruptible with incorruption."[25] Although Irenaeus' conclusions are the result of emergency reasoning rather than the systematic development of a doctrine, they show that the topic was a vital issue in the theological debates of the second century.

The controversy over the nature of the glorified body continued for a century after Irenaeus. Tertullian (A.D. 200), a lawyer who became a leader of the North African church after his conversion, wrote extensively on this theme in his polemic *Against Marcion,* and in a separate treatise *Concerning the Resurrection of the Flesh.* Following the lead of Irenaeus, he contended vigorously for the reconstitution of the material body on the premise that only the body could die, and that consequently only the body could be resurrected.[26] His interpretation was strictly literal, rejecting any suggestion that figures of speech might have been used in the Scripture.[27]

Tertullian's teaching was somewhat confused. In treating Paul's illustration of the grain in I Corinthians 15:37, 38, he insisted on the continuity of a *body.* "Does he [Paul] not also guarantee that the resurrection shall be accomplished by that God from whom proceed all the (creatures which have served him for) examples? 'So also,' says he, 'is the resurrection of the dead.' How? Just as the grain, which is sown a body, springs up a body. This sowing of the body he called the dissolving thereof in the ground. . . . Now, just as in the case of the grain, so here: to Him will belong the work in the revival of the body, who ordered the process in the dissolution thereof."[28]

[25] *Ibid.,* V, xiii, 3.
[26] Tertullian, *Against Marcion* V, ix.
[27] Tertullian, *Concerning the Resurrection of the Flesh* XX.
[28] *Against Marcion* V, x.

Tertullian seemed to be troubled by the statement "flesh and blood cannot inherit the kingdom of God" (I Cor. 15:50), for he attempted twice to explain it, but did not make a very convincing case for his contentions. In one passage he asserted that Paul was not referring to the body itself but to the works of flesh and blood which debar men from the kingdom of God.[29] In addition, he claimed that the resurrection and the kingdom of God were different. "Not that we indeed claim the kingdom of God for the flesh: all we do is, to assert a resurrection for the substance thereof, as the gate of the kingdom through which it is entered. But the resurrection is one thing and the kingdom is another. The resurrection is first, and afterwards the kingdom. We say, therefore, that the flesh rises again, but that when changed it obtains the kingdom."[30]

The meaning of Tertullian's language is not clear. Did he intend to distinguish the resurrection from the kingdom as a state, or was he attempting to grapple with the problem of a spiritual body? Irenaeus had referred to the same passage in I Corinthians but had not drawn the same conclusion.[31] He was concerned chiefly with proving the continuity of the body, but Tertullian seems to have grasped the idea that the present body cannot enter the new state of the kingdom, and that consequently transformation must accompany or follow resurrection. He does not explain whether he thought that a lapse of time intervened between the believer's resurrection and entrance into the kingdom, or whether the sequence was logical rather than chronological. Perhaps the confusion was due to the fact that he did not comprehend the nature of the problem. In his eagerness to refute the Gnostics' position he failed to define the nature of the spiritual body, and his concept was too materialistic. It is doubtful whether he could, with his limited knowledge of the constitution of matter, have formed a definition of the "spiritual body" that

---

[29] Ibid.

[30] Ibid.

[31] Irenaeus, Against Heresies V, vii, 1, 2. See Sparrow-Simpson's excellent discussion of this point in The Resurrection and Modern Thought (New York: Longmans, Green, and Company, 1911), pp. 343-347. Simpson makes Tertullian more of a materialist than he probably was.

would not have divested it of all semblance of reality for his own thinking and have caused him to dismiss the resurrection as an illusion.

Notwithstanding this deficiency, Tertullian performed an invaluable service in dispelling certain objections to the doctrine. He refuted the allegations that the resurrection was only a symbol of moral change, or that it was purely figurative, or that it was the entrance into heaven at the moment of death.[32] Such attempts to explain away the literal significance of the Biblical teaching are not new; Tertullian met most of them seventeen centuries ago. He was impatient with the fancies and allegories of the mystics, and if he was more rigidly literal than even Scripture warranted, he erred on the side of coherence.

Contemporary with Tertullian was the Greek school of Alexandria, of which Origen was the chief representative. Like Tertullian he was a controversialist, who engaged in debate with the pagan opposition. He was nurtured in conflict, for when he was seventeen years old his father died a martyr in the persecutions of Severus (A.D. 202). Two years later he became the head of the catechetical school at Alexandria. His intellectual brilliance made him the leading scholar of his day. Six thousand written publications, of which only a fraction are known, have been attributed to his pen. Despite a few theological irregularities, Origen is classed as a defender of Christianity and as an expositor of the faith.

Origen's teaching on the resurrection appeared in his work against Celsus, a pagan, who ridiculed the supernatural element in the gospel. "Neither we, then, nor the Holy Scriptures, assert that with the same bodies, without a change to a higher condition, shall those who were long dead arise from the earth and live again; for in so speaking, Celsus makes a false charge against us."[33] "We do *not* assert, however, that God will raise men from the dead with the same flesh and blood, as has been shown in the preceding pages; for we do not maintain that the natural body,

---

[32] Tertullian, *Concerning the Resurrection of the Flesh* XIX, XX, XXII.
[33] Origen, *Against Celsus* V, xviii.

which is sown in corruption, and in dishonor, and in weakness, will rise again such as it was sown."[34]

Origen did not agree with Tertullian's literal interpretation of the resurrection, for he did not insist on the continuity of the identical bodily substance; nevertheless, he did not deny the physical nature of the resurrection body. "If it is certain that we are to make use of bodies, and if the bodies which have fallen are declared to rise again . . . , it can be a matter of doubt to no one that they rise again, in order that we may be clothed with them a second time at the resurrection."[35] Origen was more careful to stress the "spiritual" nature of the body than Tertullian had been. He stipulated that it would not be entangled with the passions of flesh and blood, but that it would be "capable of inhabiting the heavens."[36] The nature of this body, however, would be essentially corporeal, not ethereal.

We consider a spiritual body to be of such a nature as ought to be inhabited not only by all perfect souls, but also by all of those creatures which will be liberated from the slavery of corruption.
. . . the one [body] which we now make use of in a state of meanness, and corruption, and weakness, is not a different body from that which we shall possess in incorruption, and in power, and in glory; but that the same body, when it has cast away the infirmities in which it is now entangled, shall be transmuted into a condition of glory, being rendered spiritual. . . .[37]

While Tertullian stressed the material continuity of the resurrection body and Origen emphasized the transformation into a spiritual body, both agreed on the reality of the resurrection. Origen did not dismiss it as illusory, though his concept was somewhat less mechanical. Both of these men proclaimed a guarantee of hope beyond the present life and a material transformation which all Christians would ultimately experience. Sparrow-Simpson points out that neither Tertullian nor Origen owed his

[34] *Ibid.*, VI, xxix.
[35] Origen, *De Principiis* II, x, 1, 2.
[36] *Ibid.*
[37] *Ibid.*, III, vi, 4, 6.

belief to speculation, but that each based it on the interpretation of Paul's words in I Corinthians 15.[38] Although they differed in conclusions, they acknowledged the authority of Scripture, and both appealed to the same source.

The formulations of the doctrine which they produced in answer to the pressures of heretical perversion and of pagan denial have persisted to the present day. Among those who believe in the corporeal resurrection the Fathers' emphases on the material and spiritual aspects are still traceable, as are the objections of their opponents. The affirmation that Jesus rose bodily from the dead on the third day, and that consequently all believers will rise when He appears, is written into the major Christian creeds. It has been the faith of martyrs and missionaries and is the core of evangelical preaching.

[38] *Op. cit.*, pp. 343-353.

VI   *The Historical*
Evidences

Although true faith is essentially a voluntary affirmation independent of proof, the Scriptures nowhere demand committal
without some reasonable basis. Between the extremes of gullibility
and of chronic skepticism there is a middle ground of belief which
may transcend the limitations of scientific logic, but which begins with historic facts. The frequent repetition of the material
circumstances of the resurrection indicates that the disciples of
Jesus accepted what had initially seemed incredible because they
found that His predictions were supported by the events that
followed His death. However these occurrences may be explained
in the framework of modern psychology, they were convincing to
the Lord's immediate associates, some of whom were as little disposed to believe that He would rise as is the most skeptical
materialist today.

The Certainty of Jesus' Death

One of the striking features of the Passion narrative is its
emphasis on the certainty of Jesus' death. Although the details of
crucifixion are sketched only in outline, each of the Gospels
devotes at least two paragraphs to the fact of His death and to the
burial. They stress the *fact* much more than the *manner* or the
process.

It may be that the Gospel writers took for granted that their readers would be familiar with crucifixion, which was a common Roman method of capital punishment, and that a full description of the phenomena would be either superfluous or revolting. On the other hand, their selection of material must be considered in relation to their objective. They intended to convey clearly to their readers that the cross was not the end of Jesus' career, for they worshiped Him as a living Lord, not as a dead martyr. Nevertheless, the fact of death was a necessary prerequisite to the resurrection, for if Jesus did not really die, He could not have risen from the dead.

Though the foregoing statement may seem trite or labored, it is not superfluous. Recent attacks on the verity of Christianity have suggested that Jesus' death was either feigned or a mistaken impression drawn from a lapse into unconsciousness. Close logic demands a careful examination of the witnesses to His death.

Although the four Gospels may differ in their accounts of the events at the crucifixion, they agree in almost identical words that Jesus actually died. Mark says, "[he] gave up the ghost" (15:37); Matthew, "[he] yielded up his spirit" (27:50); Luke, "he gave up the ghost" (23:46); John, "he . . . gave up his spirit" (19:30) . If one adds to these statements the numerous declarations of the Acts and Epistles that "Christ died . . . ," there is unanimous agreement by the earliest witnesses.

Within the Gospel narratives are more detailed testimonies to support the foregoing quotations. The first witness was the centurion who commanded the execution squad at Calvary. He was probably a man of superior intelligence, for centurions in the Roman army were usually experienced soldiers, selected from the ranks on the basis of alertness and ability. Through his experiences on the battlefield and at executions the centurion became an expert in the grim art of killing and would have known whether Jesus had merely fainted or had actually expired. His comment, "Truly this man was the Son of God" (Mark 15:39) , shows by the tense of the verb *was* that, in his judgment, Jesus was dead.

John does not repeat the verdict of the centurion but preserves the story of the piercing of Jesus' side. Because the Passover Sabbath began late on Friday afternoon, the Jewish authorities had requested of Pilate that the bodies be removed lest their hanging in public view should incur ceremonial defilement. According to Roman custom, victims were usually left on the cross until they expired, and often the bodies were allowed to remain afterward as a warning to other offenders. If they were not already dead, the executioners broke their legs to hasten the end, or to cripple them should they survive. John states that the soldiers intended to follow this procedure at the crucifixion of Jesus. When they came to Him, they found that He was dead already. As a test they pierced His side with a spear, and "straightway there came out blood and water" (John 19:34). The separation of the dark-red corpuscles from the thin whitish serum of the blood indicated that death had previously taken place.

When Joseph of Arimathea requested the body for burial (Matt. 27:57, 58) Pilate summoned the centurion for confirmation of Jesus' decease. Since men frequently lived on a cross as long as three days, the governor feared that the petition might be a subterfuge. He accepted the word of the centurion as official certification that the execution had been completed. The Gospel statement (Mark 15:43, 44) plainly implies that Pilate would not have relinquished the body if there had been any doubt about Jesus' death.

Of the multitude of persons who passed along the road to Calvary on that fateful morning the Gospels mention one outstanding group—the women. Probably not many of the Twelve were present. Matthew and Mark say that they had fled at the time of the arrest in Gethsemane (Matt. 26:56; Mark 14:50), although John and Peter followed to the trial in the chambers of the high priest (John 18:15, 16). The women stayed together and were near the cross when Jesus breathed His last. In their group were Mary, Jesus' mother, her sister Salome, Mary of Cleopas, and Mary Magdalene. Not only did they witness His suffering and death, but they followed the body as it was taken down from the cross, and watched the burial in Joseph's garden (Matt. 27:61; Mark 15:47; Luke 23:55). The four Gospels aver that on the morning of the first day of the week these same women came to the tomb, bearing spices to complete the preparation of the body for burial. Had they been unsure of His death, they would not have undertaken so disagreeable and dangerous a mission.

The final witness to the actuality of Jesus' death was the burial party composed of Joseph of Arimathea and Nicodemus. Joseph of Arimathea was a wealthy member of the Sanhedrin, the highest council of the Jewish nation, who had become a follower of Jesus (Matt. 27:57; Mark 15:43; Luke 23:50, 51; John 19:38). Nicodemus, who assisted him, was "the teacher of Israel" (John 3:10), and also a member of the council (7:50). These men would have discerned the difference between a comatose body and a corpse. They could scarcely have handled Jesus' remains without knowing whether there was still life in them or not. If there had been even the faintest evidence of animation, they would not have embalmed Him and buried Him in a tomb.

A consideration of the evidence leaves no room for doubt that Jesus died. The skilled observer, the physical results of the spear-thrust, the official pronouncement of the government, the obvious intention of the women who came to the tomb, and the committal by His aristocratic friends remove any possibility of illusion or deceit.

An important question remains. What became of the body? It could not have been brought out of a coma; it could not have been revived by the action of the disciples; it did not remain in the tomb long enough to disintegrate and disappear into dust; and yet it can be traced by the continuity of observation from the cross to the last resting-place in the garden. The only acceptable conclusion is that something mysterious and magnificent happened on the morning of the third day to cancel the work of death and to transform the fleshly organism into the instrument of glory.

The verity of so stupendous an event as the resurrection of Christ should not be dependent upon mere hearsay or upon subjective opinion. If it is the basis for a faith which alters the course of human decisions and which becomes the ground of assurance of eternal life, it must have some qualifications for commending itself to the acceptance of intelligent men. Historic proofs cannot compel belief, but they can facilitate it by showing that the words or deeds which call for faith are inherently probable. Faith is fixed on the Person of Christ, not solely on the events; but if the events are real, so is the Person who caused them.

The doctrine of the physical resurrection of Christ would not have been propounded had it not been believed fully by the disciples who first preached it. To assert that Jesus of Nazareth was alive after His crucifixion would be an extremely dangerous statement to make in Jerusalem during the first few weeks after His death, since it would alarm His enemies and evoke their vengeful wrath. He had been executed on the charge of insurrection against Rome, and if He were still at large, those who knew of His whereabouts would be under grave suspicion of promoting a conspiracy.

Furthermore, if He had risen from the dead, His enemies were thereby put in the position of having killed their Messiah—a charge which the early preachers of the church did not hesitate to make (Acts 2:23, 36; 3:14, 15; 4:10; 5:30, 31; 7:52). To voice such an accusation publicly without sufficient evidence to support it would be foolhardy. Why should these followers of Jesus have risked imprisonment and death for a lost cause? Why should they have asserted that Jesus had risen if their opponents could prove that He was still in the tomb? The evidence must have been strong enough from the beginning to make the case for Christian faith unshakable.

The positive evidence for the resurrection may be divided into three categories: (1) the material facts concerning the displaced stone, the empty tomb, and the graveclothes; (2) the physical appearances of Christ described by numerous witnesses; and (3) the historical results, which include the personal transformation of the disciples, the advent of the Holy Spirit, and the origin and growth of the Christian church. From the study of these phenomena one may attain a fair conclusion concerning what actually happened to the body of Jesus. The records, though in some instances fragmentary, are nevertheless independent. They bear every mark of being the product of individual writers who either were eyewitnesses or had access to the reports of eyewitnesses. No one of them possessed a complete knowledge of all facts involved, but their cumulative testimony is too direct and too sincere to be set aside as hallucination or fabrication. On the cardinal facts the accounts coincide, and where differences occur they can be explained by the emotional state or by the circumstances of the witnesses.

The evidences for the resurrection fitted naturally into the framework of the disciples' life in the forty days between the crucifixion and the ascension and were incidental to their current procedure, though these experiences modified that procedure when their significance was realized. For instance, the women discovered that the tomb was empty when they went to anoint the body of Jesus; they were not summoned by an alarm because the body had vanished. The appearance of Jesus to the disciples in the upper room occurred while they were assembled to discuss plans based on the assumption that He was forever removed from their world; they were not conducting a séance to establish contact with Him. The astonishment which the evidence evoked, and the subsequent change in the disciples' thinking, proved that the events of the forty days were unanticipated and were consequently not manufactured to fit the occasion.

The Material Evidence

The Displaced Stone

The material evidence for the resurrection deals with the physical facts that were immediately apparent to contemporary observers. The first and most obvious of these was the displaced stone. Many of the tombs in Palestine were hollowed out of soft limestone rock, leaving a low doorway for access. Outside the doorway and parallel to the wall of the tomb, a narrow inclined groove was cut in which was set on edge a large circular stone, usually weighing not less than a ton. While the tomb was vacant, the stone was held at one side by a cleat or small block placed beneath it. After a body was placed in the tomb, the cleat was removed, and the stone settled into place, covering the door completely. Because of its weight it could be rolled back only by the united effort of several strong men, and it made an effective barrier against vandalism or robbery.

All four Gospels agree that the tomb of Joseph was closed in conventional fashion. Matthew (27:60) alone states that the stone was rolled against the door, but the others speak of its removal, which is a tacit admission that it had been placed in position. It could not have been moved by the women, nor could the disciples have moved it without bringing together a group large enough to make secrecy improbable.

Matthew adds that the chief priests and Pharisees demanded sealing of the tomb by the Roman government. Recalling the prediction of Jesus that He would rise from the dead (John 2:19), and fearing that His disciples might attempt to steal the body in order to simulate fulfillment of His words, they asked for official action. Matthew's account of Pilate's reply is ambiguous. Pilate did not take full responsibility for closing the tomb or for appointing a guard. "Ye have a guard," he said; "go, make it as sure as ye can" (Matt. 27:65). It is possible that Pilate sent a delegate with them to seal the stone, if that meaning can be read into "Ye have a guard." It is more likely that he was eager to dismiss the case, and that he was brushing the Jews off by telling them to make their own seal and to appoint their own guard from the Temple police (27:65, 66).

Either alternative, however, guarantees that the tomb could not have been opened without incurring the serious risk of immediate detection and prosecution. If the seal were only that of the Sanhedrin, they had the knowledge and consent of Pilate to support them. A handful of disorganized disciples, or the timid coterie of women could scarcely have removed the body if it were watched by an armed band. Matthew also asserts that the removal of the stone was witnessed by the guards, who were terrified by the angelic messenger, and that they immediately hastened into the city to report the weird occurrence to the chief priests (28:11, 12).

When the women reached the garden early on the first day of the week, the stone had already been rolled aside. Matthew (28:2), writing from the standpoint of the guard, says that an angel removed it. Mark (16:3) recounts the debate which the women held among themselves, wondering how they would remove the stone, which they knew had been set in place. They were surprised to find that it had been moved, and that there was ready access to the burial chamber. Luke (24:2) follows the same line of thought, "they found the stone rolled away from the tomb." John (20:1) agrees, though he mentions only Mary Magdalene by name.

The witnesses, therefore, agree unanimously that (1) Jesus was buried in a tomb hollowed out of living rock; (2) a large circular stone was rolled in front of it; (3) the women realized that if they were to complete their sad errand somebody would have to open the door of the tomb; (4) they did not expect to find it open; and (5) when they did, the discovery was a distinct shock to them. If the disciples had plotted to remove the body, as the Sanhedrin had feared, the women had no knowledge of their plan. Certainly they had not the strength to accomplish such a task themselves, nor had they anticipated an attempt.

The disciples could not have opened the tomb without becoming involved in an armed clash with the guard. Even if they had forced their way into the sepulchre, their action would have been reported to the authorities and would have been cause for immediate arrest and prosecution. The excuse of the guards, "His disciples came by night, and stole him away while we slept" (Matt. 28:13), was patently false. If the guards were asleep, how did they know what happened? If their charge could be proved, why were not the disciples seized and questioned? How could a small body of men have engaged in a fight and then have carried off the corpse of a full-grown man without having been noticed by at least one person? Finally, if Joseph of Arimathea had placed the body in his private garden, how could this action take place without his knowledge, and without interrogation by the Pharisees? Since they knew where the body had been placed, why did they pursue their investigation no further? If, as Matthew (28:12-14) says, they were merely creating a rumor to screen the truth that Jesus had risen, and to cover their own confusion, the narrative becomes coherent. The power of God had intervened to break the seal, and the stone was rolled aside by a divine hand to give mute witness that "the man of mystery had gone his way."[1]

The Empty Tomb

A second aspect of the material witness is that the tomb was empty. The Gospels agree that the body had disappeared. Matthew's narrative says, "And the angel answered. . . . He is not here; for he is risen, even as he said. Come, see the place where the Lord lay" (28:5, 6). The imperfect tense of *lay* (Gr. *ekeito,* "was lying," or "used to lie") implies that the body had been laid on the stone shelf inside the tomb but was no longer there. The Markan account is substantially like that of Matthew. Luke differs by stating that the women "entered in, and found not the body of the Lord Jesus" (Luke 24:3) before the angelic messengers explained the reason for its absence (24:4-8). John gives the impression that Mary Magdalene's report of the absence of Jesus' body preceded her investigation of the interior of the tomb (20:1, 2). She saw that the stone had been removed, and consequently concluded that the body was gone. Peter and John, who followed her, actually looked inside, and corroborated her deduction.

The uniform testimony that the tomb was untenanted is strong confirmation of the resurrection. If the stone had been rolled aside by accident, or if an intruder had been interrupted in the act of robbing the tomb, the body would still have remained in its place. Since the body was not there, it must have been removed. But how? A corpse is not an easy object to transport for any distance, or to conceal. More than one person would have been needed to carry it away, and in multiplying assistants the likelihood of secrecy would have lessened. It is almost incredible

---

[1] Epigram by Edwin Markham.

that Jesus' body could have been spirited away to another burial place either by Joseph of Arimathea or by the disciples without some hint, dropped accidentally or intentionally.

The unfeigned surprise and concern of the disciples are good proof that they neither anticipated a removal nor were a party to it. Psychologically such action was impossible, for they were too disorganized by sorrow and too fearful of the authorities to attempt the venture. At the betrayal in the garden of Gethsemane "all the disciples left him, and fled" (Matt. 26:56). When they met again after His death they convened behind locked doors (John 20:19) "for fear of the Jews." They were not ready to initiate so bold a coup as the rescue of Jesus' body from the custody of armed police. Since they did not understand Jesus' prediction of His resurrection, they could not anticipate it and would be quite content to leave His body in Joseph's care, for they could scarcely find a better place. Transfer and reinterment would have been farthest from their thoughts.

The enemies of Jesus would not be likely to disturb the body, for their interests would be served best by leaving it in a fixed and well-known grave. If He had predicted resurrection, they could always refute His claim by pointing to an acknowledged burial place. Such, indeed, was their purpose in setting the watch. If He did not rise in three days, He would not rise at all, and their verdict would be justified.

Kirsopp Lake suggests that the evidence of the empty tomb is inconclusive because the women did not visit the place where Jesus was actually buried.

It is seriously a matter for doubt whether the women were really in a position to be quite certain that the tomb which they visited was that in which they had seen Joseph of Arimathea bury the Lord's body. The neighborhood of Jerusalem is full of rock tombs, and it would not be easy to distinguish one from another without careful notes. . . . It is very doubtful if they were close to the tomb at the moment of burial. . . . It is likely that they were watching from a distance, and that Joseph of Arimathea was a representative of the Jews rather than of the disciples. If so, they would have had but a limited power to distinguish between one rock tomb and another close to it. The possibility, therefore, that they came to the wrong tomb is to be reckoned with, and it is important because it supplies the natural explanation of the fact that whereas they had seen the tomb closed, they found it open. . . .

If it were not the same, the circumstances all seem to fall into line. The women came in the early morning to a tomb which they thought was the one in which they had seen the Lord buried. They expected to find a closed tomb, but they found an open one; and a young man . . . guessing their errand, tried to tell them that they had made a mistake in the place. "He is not here," said he, "see the place where they laid him," and probably pointed to the next tomb. But the women were frightened at the detection of their errand, and fled. . . .[2]

Lake concludes his discussion by saying, "The empty tomb is for us doctrinally indefensible and historically insufficiently accredited."

This objection will not bear close scrutiny. The Gospels, as Lake admits, state emphatically that the women witnessed the burial of Jesus and noted the exact spot where His body was laid to rest (Matt. 27:61; Mark 15:47; Luke 23:55). Had the tomb been one of many in a public burying ground, it is conceivable that in the semi-darkness of early dawn and under the emotional stress of the unusual situation the women could have become confused. Since, however, the interment was in a private garden, they could scarcely have been mistaken. There were several present at the burial, and not all of them would have forgotten the true location in three days' time. Furthermore, the tomb was presumably the only one in the garden, and there would have been no alternative choice.

Lake fails to explain why the "young man" would have been present either in a public cemetery or in a private garden at such an early hour. What conceivable motive would have drawn a stranger there? If he were not a stranger, but one of the disciples, conducting an independent investigation, why should his presence have terrorized the women? Mark's account, on which Lake relies, states that he was seated *inside* the tomb, so that he could

[2] Kirsopp Lake, *The Historical Evidence for the Resurrection of Jesus Christ* (New York: G. P. Putnam's Sons, 1907), pp. 250-253.

scarcely have meant that they were at the wrong place when he said (Mark 16:6), "behold, the place where they laid him!" The main implication of his invitation was not that the women had come to the wrong place, but that Jesus was no longer there; they could see where He had been laid, but the body had vanished.

Finally, the empty tomb cannot be explained by the normal disintegration of the body. Decay would only have begun in three days' time and would not have reached the stage of complete chemical dissolution. To assume that the body of Jesus evaporated into gases within three days of death is to project a miracle almost as great as the resurrection itself. G. D. Yarnold, in his recent work *Risen Indeed*,[3] suggests that the material body of the Lord ceased to exist, or was annihilated. The presence of the scars on the Lord's body does not accord with his theory, but in any case Yarnold is compelled to conclude that the tomb was empty.

The Graveclothes

Another important factor in the material witness is the state of the graveclothes. When Joseph, with Nicodemus' assistance, took the body from the cross, he carried it quickly to the garden, where he "wrapped [Gr. *enetulixen*] it in a clean linen cloth, and laid it in his own new tomb" (Matt. 27:59-60). Mark's language is almost identical, though he says, "wound [*eneilēsen*] him in the linen cloth" (Mark 15:46). Luke (23:53) corroborates these statements, using the same word as Matthew. John says that Joseph and Nicodemus "bound" (Gr. *edēsan*) His body in "swathes" or "bandages" (Gr. *othoniois*), using about one hundred pounds of spices, which Nicodemus furnished. He specifies that they followed the usual burial custom of the Jews in the wrapping of the corpse (John 19:39, 40).

Is the difference between the Johannine and Synoptic accounts significant? The pressure under which Joseph and Nicodemus were acting would favor a hasty wrapping of the body in a single linen sheet, which would not consume much time. On the

---

[3] G. D. Yarnold, *Risen Indeed* (London: Oxford University Press, 1959), p. 22.

other hand, the author of the Fourth Gospel seems to have been well acquainted with Nicodemus (3:1, 7:50, 19:39), from whom he probably derived this information. The "linen cloth" may very well have been a general term, while the "swathes" or "bandages" are more specific names for the materials used in the cerements.

In preparing a body for burial according to Jewish custom, it was usually washed and straightened, and then bandaged tightly from the armpits to the ankles in strips of linen about a foot wide. Aromatic spices, often of a gummy consistency, were placed between the wrappings or folds. They served partially as a preservative and partially as a cement to glue the cloth wrappings into a solid covering. When the body was thus encased, a square piece of cloth was wrapped around the head and tied under the chin to keep the lower jaw from sagging. John's term "bound" (Gr. *edēsan*), is in perfect accord with the language of Luke 23:53, where the writer says that the body was *rolled* (literal translation of *enetulixen*) in linen. John uses the same verb to describe the head cloth, which was found "rolled up in a place by itself" (John 20:7). The language implies that the body of Jesus was not carelessly entombed, although Joseph may not have been able to complete all of the fine requirements of preparation. Had he done so, the women would not have come to the tomb on the morning after the Sabbath.

The procedure is confirmed by the account of the raising of Lazarus (John 11:44). His body appeared in the doorway of the tomb "bound hand and foot with grave-clothes [Gr. *dedemenos . . . keiriais*]; and his face was bound about with a napkin [*soudariōi*]." The words "bound" and "napkin" are the same that are used in describing Jesus' burial. If Lazarus were "bound hand and foot," so that he had to be specially released, the same method was doubtlessly employed in the burial of Jesus.

On the morning of the first day of the week the body of Jesus had vanished, but the graveclothes were still there. Neither Matthew nor Mark mentions them specifically in the account of the first visit to the tomb. Their presence may be implied in the angel's words, "Come, see the place where the Lord lay" (Matt.

28:6; cf. Mark 16:6), for unless some marker were left it would
be impossible to tell where the body had been deposited. A plain
stone slab would carry no visible impression. John corroborates
this deduction by his statement that Mary Magdalene, on her
second visit to the tomb, saw "two angels in white sitting, one
at the head, and one at the feet, where the body of Jesus had
lain" (John 20:12). While custom may have usually decreed the
position in which a body was laid, the presence of graveclothes
would make it unmistakable. This implication becomes a certainty in the statement that the unnamed disciple and Simon
Peter both saw the clothes in the tomb (20:4-9; Luke 24:12).

A careful examination of the Johannine narrative shows that
the author attached considerable importance to this evidence. In
describing the hurried trip of Peter and John to the sepulchre,
he uses three distinct verbs for *see* in relation to the graveclothes.
In the sequence of the action, the unnamed disciple, presumably
John himself, reached the tomb first. Having heard from Mary
Magdalene that the body had been removed, he proceeded to in-
vestigate on his own behalf. Bending down to look in through the
dark doorway, he could see the outline of the linen graveclothes
lying on the shelf. Satisfied that the body must still be there, even
though the tomb had been opened, he withdrew to await Peter,
who had been following him. He "saw" (*blepei*) the clothes in
the same way that he would "see" anything else. His eyes registered that they were visible, and consequently real. The observation was casual, but not inaccurate.

Peter arrived in a few seconds and did not content himself with
a cautious glance at the tomb from the outside. Unhesitatingly
he entered the sepulchre and stood there gazing at the clothes.
The verb translated "seeth" (Gr. *theorei*) implies careful observation, watching for the purpose of apprehending the significance
of an object or event. Peter evidently stood for several moments
in silent contemplation of the graveclothes—long enough to make
his partner wonder why Peter should be spending so much time
within the tomb when he, the first comer, had been able to satisfy his curiosity with a glance.

Why should the condition of the graveclothes excite Peter's

amazement? The Fourth Gospel specifies that they were lying just where they were when the body was in them, and that "the napkin . . . was . . . not lying with the linen cloths, but rolled up in a place by itself" (John 20:7). Why should this arrangement have seemed peculiar?

There is a strong hint that the clothes were not folded as if Jesus had unwound them and then deposited them in two neat piles on the shelf. The word used to describe the napkin or head cloth does not connote a flat folded square like a table napkin, but a ball of cloth bearing the appearance of being rolled around an object that was no longer there. The wrappings were in position where the body had lain, and the head cloth was where the head had been, separated from the others by the distance from armpits to neck. The shape of the body was still apparent in them, but the flesh and bone had disappeared.

If this hypothesis be correct, and it seems to follow the facts, how was the corpse extricated from the wrappings, since they would not slip over the curves of the body when tightly wound around it? No robbers would ever have rewound the wrappings in their original shape, for there would not have been time to do so. They would have flung the cloths down in disorder and fled with the body. Fear of detection would have made them act as hastily as possible.

While Peter was cogitating over this puzzle, the other disciple entered the tomb. The account says that "he saw, and believed" (20:8). The word "saw" (Gr. *eidon*) implies mental perception or realization as well as physical sight. In modern language, he "clicked." The answer to the enigma was that Jesus had risen, passing through the graveclothes, which He left undisturbed as a silent proof that death could not hold Him, nor material bonds restrain Him.

The Lukan testimony to Peter's visit (Luke 24:12) is uncertain, for it is omitted by the Western text of Codex D, the Old Latin versions, and Marcion, and seems to duplicate the language of John 20:5. It does, however, occur in the text of Aleph and B, two of the oldest uncial manuscripts, and in the "Caesarean text" of Theta. If it is a subsequent addition from John, it represents an early tradition similar to the numerous other "interpolations" that occur in the last few chapters of Luke. Its presence is not necessary to the foregoing argument, nor does its absence detract from it.

The interpretation of these phenomena compels the candid reader to admit that the sudden disappearance of Jesus' body is a mystery not easily resolved by ordinary explanations. The theory of theft was propounded by the Jewish Sanhedrin,[4] and was held by their successors, but it is not adequate to account for the presence of the graveclothes, nor was it coherent as reported by the guard. If, on the other hand, the reality of the resurrection be conceded, can it be reconciled with the known laws of physics? Jesus had unquestionably died, and had passed beyond the possibility of resuscitation from suspended animation. Since the process of death had already begun, as the "blood and water" (19:34) showed, He could not by any ordinary standards have returned to life. It is a truism of the medical profession that if a man is pronounced dead and subsequently regains consciousness, the original diagnosis was incorrect. If Jesus did return to life, some new potency must have operated in Him that not only arrested decay but restored His body to its normal functions.

Again, if His body passed through the graveclothes and through encircling walls without disturbing the organization of either, there must have been some change in its physical constitution. No ordinary man can try to walk through a wall or through a closed door without leaving some visible effects both upon the wall and upon himself. Nevertheless, after the resurrection Jesus appeared and disappeared at will (Luke 24:15, 16, 31, 36; John 20:19, 26), whether on the open roadway where any person approaching could be seen from a distance, or within a room, the door of which was closed and barred.

The Gospel writers formulated no scientific theories to explain the resurrection. Research had not advanced sufficiently in their day to permit hypotheses of the constitution of matter that would provide a reasoned basis for such a phenomenon. Their non-

---

[4] See Matt. 28:11-15.

scientific approach confirms their truthfulness, for since they could record only what they had seen, they could not have fabricated the event to fit a preconceived theory. If the various accounts seem disconnected and desultory, they reflect the artless honesty of men who endeavored to describe a unique experience in factual terms, and who were not sophisticated enough to invent a "scientific" explanation.

The apostles did not attribute the resurrection to magic or to necromancy; nor are there in the Biblical accounts superstitious allusions to witchcraft such as characterized similar narratives in the Middle Ages. On the contrary, the Gospels dismiss the thought that these material happenings were the result of hallucinations or the idle dreams of superstitious minds. The disciples themselves were critical of the initial reports and refused to take them seriously (Luke 24:11, 23, 24, 41; John 20:25). They were unwilling to accept the testimony concerning the empty tomb unless they could see Jesus for themselves. Only when the material evidence was supplemented by direct contact with the living Lord did they acknowledge the fact that He had truly risen.

Recent research has supplied two possible ways of accounting for the physical accompaniments, though neither can be established conclusively. The atomic theory of matter propounded by modern physics and generally accepted by scientists contends that matter is not a solid impenetrable block, but that it is composed of points of force in constant motion which are organized by well-defined patterns. These "points," or electrons, neutrons, protons, etc., are comparable to a solar system, in which one revolves about the other with an appreciable space between them. Thousands of these tiny systems or atoms constitute the molecules which, in turn, make up the various types of matter, whether it be organic, like living tissue, or inorganic, like metal, stone, or plastic. Each has its own particular pattern of forces, operating in its own way.

The visible shape of matter may be identical for various materials. For instance, a human body could be duplicated in wax so that if it were motionless, the original would be hardly distinguishable from the copy. The properties of the two, however, would be different, since flesh is living and animate, while wax is dead and inert. Flesh has power of self-locomotion; wax does not. It is conceivable that a body could be composed of matter in an even more animated state, so that its functioning would be on a higher and different level. If its atomic organization were of such a pattern that it could interlace with the pattern of other matter, a body so structured of one kind of matter could pass through a wall of the other without leaving a trace. Perhaps the resurrection body of Jesus was so constituted that it could penetrate other matter without becoming disarranged or disorganized itself.

A somewhat different explanation of the resurrection is based on its possible relation to the concept of dimension. To a person living in a world of only two dimensions, length and breadth with no height or depth, any stranger moving through that world in a third dimension would be seen only as footprints alternately appearing and disappearing. His three-dimensional bulk would be invisible, and the phenomena of the disappearing footprints would be quite inexplicable. He would be a perennial miracle to the inhabitants of Flatland.

If someone could step out of the eternal world into ours, his advent, career, and ultimate return to the heavenly country would be one constant marvel. He could become visible or invisible at will, changing his relation to suit his convenience or desire in much the same fashion as Jesus appeared and vanished during the period of forty days before His ascension. While this explanation is wholly hypothetical, it possesses a degree of plausibility and is definitely connected with the concept of realities which are not perceivable by ordinary instruments.

The foregoing theories are not proffered as final, nor is there any intention of minimizing the divine aspect of the resurrection by a pseudoscientific explanation. The concepts of atomic interchange and of a fourth dimension are at best only analogies or illustrations of a different category of being which transcends the ordinary plane of living, though it may intersect the phenomenal world of space and time. Unquestionably, the physical evidences of the resurrection mark an event which belongs to this world but did not originate in it. The resurrection of Christ is an integral part of history although it cannot be accounted for by purely natural causes. The displaced stone, the vacant tomb, and the empty graveclothes are the eloquent witnesses that one life has been able to overcome death, and to leave its imprint on the material world.

The Physical Appearances

The case for the validity of the resurrection, founded upon the genuineness and accuracy of Jesus' predictions and upon the facts of the empty tomb and the graveclothes, would be incomplete without the direct witness of His personal appearances. Deductions from the material evidence might confirm the probability of the event but would not make it a reality to the disciples. As one of them stated, "And certain of them that were with us went to the tomb, and found it even so as the women had said: but him they saw not" (Luke 24:24). The failure to establish personal contact with the risen Lord left them in doubt concerning the interpretation of the material evidence. Some further confirmation was needed to make its message convincing.

The acuteness of this problem was recognized by the first preachers of the Christian church. From the outset they had to contend with the false rumor spread by the Jewish rulers that Jesus' disciples stole His body while the soldiers slept. (Matt. 28:11-15). Inconsistent as it was, the disciples could not combat it easily unless they had some positive experience to offer as a refutation. Confronting a learned and hostile hierarchy who had opposed Jesus bitterly during His lifetime, the apostles did not dare to make indefensible assertions. To claim falsely that Jesus had risen from the dead would expose them to ridicule and would invite disaster to their cause. They were too astute to offer to the public baseless legends or wild dreams as the initial proof of their new faith.

Eleven manifestations of Jesus are cited in the Gospels and Epistles as evidence for the resurrection. They differ widely in time, setting, persons involved, and results. They agree unanimously, however, that His physical presence was attested by competent witnesses, who were willing to stake their lives on the fact that He had risen.

According to the Fourth Gospel Mary Magdalene was the first to meet the living Lord. In company with other women she had set out for Joseph's garden, carrying spices to complete the anointing of Jesus' body after the hasty burial. In their nervous excitement and eagerness they had failed to arrange for access to the tomb, and while they hurried through the dim streets they debated how they would obtain entrance. As they approached the site, they perceived that the sepulchre was already open. A comparison of the Gospel records suggests that Mary Magdalene, observing that the stone had been rolled from the door and fearing that the body had been removed, rushed away to inform the disciples (John 20:1, 2). Her companions remained at the tomb for further investigation (Matt. 28:11; Mark 16:1-4; Luke 24:1-3, 10).

Mary's disconcerting news aroused the disciples, two of whom immediately visited the tomb (John 20:3-10). Finding no trace of Jesus except the empty graveclothes, they concurred in her apprehension concerning the body but could add no positive evidence.

In the meantime, Mary slowly retraced her steps to the garden, drawn by an irresistible desire to visit the place where she had last seen her Lord. Peering through the doorway with tear-filled eyes, she spied two angels who inquired the cause of her sorrow. As she explained mournfully the reason for her errand, she became aware of a person standing behind her. Assuming that it was the gardener, she questioned him, hoping for a solution to the mystery.

Calling her by name, the stranger revealed that he was Jesus. With intense emotion she flung her arms around His feet, as if to hold Him forever. Quietly and firmly He said, "Cease clinging to me! I have not yet made my final ascent to the Father. Go, and tell my brethren that I am still here" (20:17, paraphrased).

Mary's reaction was the natural recoil of surprise, followed by the ecstasy of realization. Recognition was not immediate because she did not expect to see Him, and because her tears obscured her vision. Had Jesus been surrounded by an aura of glory or had He spoken in tones of thunder, she would have known Him instantly. She mistook Him for the gardener because nothing in His garb or bearing suggested a supernatural visitor.

On the other hand, it seems scarcely possible that Mary's sorrow and confusion could have prevented the recognition of one whom she had seen alive so recently. It is more likely that the changed appearance of the resurrection body would have been the obstacle. Just as a lapse of time alters the face of an old friend so that he seems unfamiliar until he introduces himself by voice and manner, the resurrection had changed Jesus. The difference in His appearance was enough to prevent instant recognition, but the continuity of personality assured His identity.

The women who had accompanied Mary Magdalene also saw the risen Christ. The Synoptic accounts (Matt. 28:1-10; Mark 16:1-8; Luke 24:1-11) differ in some details but agree generally that they entered the tomb and were astounded to find angelic visitants, who conveyed the message that Jesus would join His disciples in Galilee. Overcome by fear, the women fled in panic. Matthew adds the comment that Jesus Himself greeted them as they went to inform the disciples. They seem to have recognized Him more easily than did Mary, perhaps because they were less preoccupied with their own sorrow. Their reaction was like hers for, "they came and took hold of his feet, and worshipped him" (Matt. 28:9). To them also He was tangible, and therefore real.

A private interview with Peter is included in the series which Paul enumerates in I Corinthians 15. The conversation is not recorded, but there are other references that substantiate the event. Mark quotes the angels' command to the women as follows: ". . . tell his disciples *and Peter,* He goeth before you into Galilee" (Mark 16:7, italics ours). Luke also alludes to a personal appearance which must have taken place on the first day (Luke 24:34). Singling out Peter from the others shows that Jesus had marked him for special attention. Probably He dealt with His vacillating disciple about the denial and cleared away the sense of alienation and loss which had enshrouded him with despair. This contact with the living Lord confirmed the mute testimony of the graveclothes and rendered Peter's joyous announcement to his colleagues remarkably convincing. A reflection of this encounter appears in his subsequent teaching, "Blessed be the God and Father of our Lord Jesus Christ, who according to his great mercy begat us again unto a living hope by the resurrection of Jesus Christ from the dead . . ." (I Pet. 1:3).

The meeting of Jesus with two lesser-known disciples was recorded in detail by Luke (24:13-35). While Cleopas and his companion were walking toward Emmaus, a village about seven miles distant from Jerusalem,[5] they were conversing about the shocking reversal of Jesus' fortunes. His dramatic arrival in Jerusalem, climaxing His phenomenal career, had raised public expectation to a high pitch. During the Passover week His original and authoritative teaching and His clever overthrow of opponents' arguments made Him the focus of interest. Undoubtedly a large segment of the populace, as well as His own disciples, were sure that the opportune moment for action had arrived, and that Jesus would restore the kingdom to Israel.

The rude shock of His sudden betrayal and ignominious death blasted their hopes, leaving them dazed and disillusioned. They could not reconcile the paradox of His miraculous powers and His meek surrender to His enemies. The rumors of the empty tomb and of the angelic visitors seemed unconvincing, especially since investigation had not yet produced positive evidence that He was alive.

The theme of their discussion was so engrossing that they failed to notice the presence of another traveler. At first they did not recognize Him, for "their eyes were holden" (Luke 24:16). His question, "What communications are these that ye have one with another, as ye walk?" conveyed to them the impression that He was unfamiliar with the news. His apparent ignorance astounded

---

[5] Codex Sinaiticus reads 160 stadia, or seventeen miles. See Emil G. Kraeling, *Bible Atlas* (New York: Rand McNally & Company, 1956), p. 409. The actual site of Emmaus is disputed.

them, for Cleopas' reply indicated that even casual visitors were acquainted with recent events in Jerusalem.

The persistent stranger pressed His question further by inquiring what kind of things had happened. The disciples' answer revealed the limitation of their knowledge and spiritual experience. "The things concerning Jesus of Nazareth, who was a prophet mighty in deed and word before God and all the people. . . . But we hoped that it was he who should redeem Israel" (24:19, 21). Instead of rejoicing in the triumph of the resurrection they were overcome by the frustration of their hopes. Although there had been some reports that He was alive, these despondent disciples had dismissed them as baseless and were consequently ready to concede that the cause was lost.

Contrary to normal expectation, Jesus did not censure them for failing either to recognize Him or to take the testimony of the women seriously. In strong language, He reproved them for not believing the prophets of the Old Testament. "O foolish men, and slow of heart to believe in all that the prophets have spoken!" (24:25). The language implies that the Messianic pattern was already fixed in the divine plan and was revealed clearly enough so that the disciples should in some measure have anticipated the Passion. Instead of being disappointed they should have realized that the divine program was being fulfilled.

The interest of the two disciples increased as the stranger developed His interpretation of the Old Testament, and the familiar prophecies gradually gained a new significance. Fascinated by this mysterious teacher, they were reluctant to part with Him. When they reached Emmaus, because the afternoon was waning rapidly they offered Him the common courtesy of entertainment.

At the evening meal Jesus was accorded the place of the guest who, according to Jewish custom, offered a prayer of thanksgiving and first broke the bread. There may have been a characteristic gesture, or a familiar prayer, that revealed His identity. In the moment of recognition He vanished. Fully assured of Jesus' resurrection, and recalling the compelling force of His teaching,

Cleopas and his friend hastened back to Jerusalem to share their experience with the other disciples.

The Johannine narrative of the meeting in Jerusalem adds the pertinent comment that the doors of the room were "shut" for fear of the Jews (John 20:19). While the language does not necessarily mean that the door was locked, the uniform usage of "shut" in the New Testament connotes the effective exclusion of visitors or invaders. The disciples, fearing arrest, had taken every precaution to debar spies from their conference, and the unaccountable presence of a stranger threw them into consternation. As mysteriously as Jesus had disappeared from the supper at Emmaus He reappeared in the chamber at Jerusalem. Since He could not have entered by the door, the only reasonable alternative, which John evidently purposed to imply, is that Jesus penetrated the walls of the room and became visible.

Jesus' greeting, "Peace" (20:19, 21), was intended to remove the tension caused by His miraculous arrival. He reassured the terrified men by showing them His hands and His side, which still bore the scars of the cross. Convinced that their Lord had actually returned from death, their sorrow turned to joy and their terror to confidence.

The marks of the wounds raise the problem of the relation of the resurrection body to the physical body that had undergone death. If it were a reanimation of the original flesh, how did it acquire new powers? If it were a new creation, why should it not be free from the marks of suffering? The obvious intent of mentioning the prints of the nails and of the spear was to dispel the false idea that He was only an apparition (Luke 24:38, 39). The resurrection was not an impersonation, but the actual reappearance of the Lord. There was continuity both in appearance and in substance with the body that the disciples had previously known, yet the dynamics were changed.

Jesus demonstrated the material nature of the resurrection more convincingly by an additional test. Upon His asking the disciples whether they had any food available, they offered Him fish and honey, which He ate in their presence to prove that He was not a ghost (24:42, 43). The episode was long remembered, for Peter, preaching in the house of Cornelius several years later, recalled that they ate and drank with Him after He rose from the dead (Acts 10:41).

Thomas was absent from the company of the disciples when Jesus appeared in the upper room. John's narrative implies that he had remained in Jerusalem, and that the others maintained communication with him. Possibly he was too overwhelmed by grief to participate in further discussion of Jesus' Passion, and he was certainly unready to accept the report of His resurrection. His scientific mind demanded experimental evidence, and since he had not seen Jesus, he refused to believe. When the others assured him that they had met the Lord, he replied, "Except I shall see in his hands the print of the nails, and put my finger into the prints of the nails, and put my hand into his side, I will not believe" (John 20:25).

In spite of his vehement expression of unbelief Thomas was persuaded to join the others at their gathering on the following Sunday. The setting was identical with that of the previous week, and Jesus' manifestation was also similar, with one significant addition. Although Thomas' emphatic protest had been spoken to the disciples alone, Jesus' quotation of his words indicated that He may have been invisibly present when they were spoken. In any case, Jesus' acceptance of the challenge overwhelmed him, and his skepticism was replaced by faith and worship.

The reversal of the critical attitude of the disciples, and especially of Thomas, obviates the objection that the resurrection faith was a product of hallucination or gullibility. The disciples were in no mood to accept statements without investigation, and they were compelled to lay aside fixed prejudices in order to believe in so stupendous a miracle. Their final commitment to the proposition that Jesus arose from the dead was founded on incontrovertible experience.

Subsequent to these first six appearances in Jerusalem were others in Galilee, predicted by an angel on the resurrection day (Matt. 28:7; Mark 16:7) and confirmed by Jesus to the women (Matt. 28:8). Since the homes of the eleven apostles were in Galilee, and the Jewish authorities in Jerusalem were hostile, they probably did not remain in Jerusalem during the entire span of the forty days. While the Passover pilgrims were in the city, the disciples could mingle with them, but after the pilgrims departed, their presence would be more conspicuous. Precipitate flight would have betrayed their eagerness to leave and would have aroused suspicion. For the first week they remained in Jerusalem, possibly secreting themselves in the home of John Mark's mother or in the house of Nicodemus. Perhaps the women found a haven with Mary and Martha at Bethany. In the second week the excitement over Jesus' death would have subsided, allowing the disciples to return to Galilee unobserved.

The order of the Galilean appearances cannot be established easily. According to Paul's testimony Jesus appeared on one occasion to more than five hundred "brethren" (I Cor. 15:6). Neither the time nor the place is specified. It is unlikely that so large a crowd could have convened in Jerusalem without creating a public sensation, but in the hills of Galilee such a gathering might be almost unnoticed. Quite possibly Jesus' manifestation occurred when a larger body of disciples had assembled to hear the report of the events in Jerusalem. The cumulative value of their resultant testimony is strong. When Paul wrote I Corinthians twenty-five years after the resurrection, he declared that the majority of the witnesses were still living, which implies that he was acquainted with some of them. Perhaps a large number of them were among the converts of Pentecost or became supporters of the Galilean churches (Acts 9:31).

An interview with James, otherwise unidentified, is also mentioned by Paul, who implies that he was living when I Corinthians was written. This man could not have been James the son of Zebedee, for he was executed by Herod Agrippa I about A.D. 44 (Acts 12:2). James the Less, also called the son of Alphaeus (Matt. 10:3), seems not to have been sufficiently prominent or influential to be known by the Corinthian church. James the Lord's brother, who was moderator of the church at Jerusalem, is the most likely choice. Prior to the resurrection the brethren of the Lord were not believers (John 7:5), but James assuredly was an active Christian in the earliest years of the church (Acts 15:13; 21:18;

Gal. 1:19). Sometime after the autumn of the final year of Jesus' ministry (the Feast of Tabernacles, John 7:2) his attitude changed. Perhaps this appearance of Christ made the difference.

The apocryphal *Gospel According to the Hebrews* provides an interesting supplement to a statement of Paul.[6] "Now the Lord, when he had given the cloth unto the servant of the priest, went unto James and appeared unto him. . . ." This implies that the event occurred on the day of resurrection, but Paul seems to place it later. If James had not been a believer, it is improbable that he would have remained in Jerusalem after the Passover—if, indeed, he had been there at all. Jesus' committal of His mother to John may hint that His brothers were not immediately available to care for her. Although the chronological data of the apocryphal account may be unreliable, it nevertheless corroborates the testimony concerning an appearance to James during the forty days.

The most detailed and graphic account is contained in the epilogue of John's Gospel (John 21). The author notes that it was the third appearance to the disciples as a group, which may mean that it took place not long after their return to Galilee. Seven of the disciples—Peter, Thomas, Nathanael, James, John, and two others who may have been Philip and Andrew—met at the Sea of Galilee. The events in Jerusalem had exhausted and bewildered them, and they naturally sought some activity that would relax their nerves and restore the normal tempo of life. At Peter's suggestion they resumed their old trade of fishing, and embarked in the evening for a night on the lake.

The labor proved fruitless, and when dawn came they were still engaged in a last attempt to catch some fish. A voice from the lakeside arrested their attention: "Boys, you haven't any food, have you?" Thinking that an agent from one of the nearby fisheries wished to negotiate for their catch, they answered, "No." Back came the reply, "Cast the net on the right side of the boat, and ye shall find." The proposal was unconventional, for trained fishermen did not usually cast their nets on the right side.

[6] Quoted by Jerome, *De Viris Illustris* 2.

Prompted by desperation, they followed the suggestion and were rewarded with a loaded net that nearly swamped the boat.

When the fish were brought to shore, Jesus cooked breakfast for the weary and discouraged men. Though it is not said that He partook of the food, the material evidence confirmed their experience in Jerusalem. If they had been tempted to discount as unreal the prior appearances occurring in a strange environment and under nervous tension, there would be no doubt of Jesus' reality when He fed them in their own surroundings. The combination of physical phenomena and spiritual instruction at the lake of Galilee validates the concept that Jesus could still act and talk on the ordinary human plane as formerly, but that He could enter or leave it at will.

Matthew mentions a prearranged appearance in Galilee on a mountainside, saying, "when they saw him, they worshipped him; but some doubted" (Matt. 28:17). Evidently a few of the eleven were still incredulous either of the trustworthiness of their own senses or of the reality of Jesus' manifestation.

The last twelve verses of Mark contain a similar narrative of a final appearance to the eleven disciples, at which Jesus spoke His parting command, "Go ye into all the world, and preach the gospel to the whole creation" (Mark 16:15). The identity of this occasion with the one in Matthew seems probable, since the final commission is included in both of them. Although the manuscript evidence for the Markan origin of these verses is uncertain, they are still an early witness to the post-resurrection activity of Jesus.

The historical sequence of the Lukan narrative leaves no doubt that the last appearance of Jesus was in Jerusalem, ten days before Pentecost. The Gospel closes with the words, "and he led them out until they were over against Bethany: and he lifted up his hands, and blessed them. And it came to pass, while he blessed them, he parted from them, and was carried up into heaven" (Luke 24:50-51). The first chapter of Acts enlarges upon the event by reproducing the colloquy between Jesus and the disciples concerning His plans for their future. He outlined a plan for the age founded upon the resurrection, promising the gift of the Holy Spirit (Acts 1:5) and predicting a long program of witnessing evangelism beginning at Jerusalem and extending to the outmost bounds of earth.

Two other manifestations of the risen Christ which occurred after the ascension should be included. One of these was granted to Stephen, who at death said, "I see the heavens opened, and the Son of man standing on the right hand of God" (Acts 7:56). The vision, which did not involve the bodily presence of Jesus, might be considered subjective because it was seen only by Stephen; nevertheless, to him the sight of Christ was an objective reality.

Similar to Stephen's vision was the subsequent self-disclosure of Christ to Paul, who included it with the resurrection appearances, stating that "last of all, as to the child untimely born, he appeared to me also" (I Cor. 15:8). Did he intend to imply that his encounter with Christ was as objective as that of Peter, of James, and of the Eleven, or that their experiences were merely subjective, as some suppose Paul's was? Paul alluded to his conversion on the road to Damascus, where he and his party were prostrated by a brilliant flash of light (Acts 9:3; 22:6; 26:13). An audible voice addressed him, calling him by name (9:4, 7; 26:14). His companions realized that a voice had spoken, though they did not understand the language. The objective aspects make this episode a legitimate piece of evidence for the resurrection of Christ.

Certain common elements characterize all of the appearances. No one of the Gospel writers has an artificial or stilted presentation of the return of Jesus from the dead. Their accounts contain no grotesque exaggeration of His powers, nor any acts of exhibitionism or vengeance. The short descriptions of His manifestations treat them as a normal part of His career, so that the ministry of the forty days is no more supernatural than the preceding three and one-half years of public ministry. Although the resurrection was without precedent, it was not abnormal for Christ.

The appearances had definite objectives. Whether Jesus wanted to reclaim Peter, dispel Thomas' doubts, dry Mary's tears, or give

extensive teaching to the Eleven, He made each occasion purposeful. He did not reveal Himself simply to evoke amazement
or applause. As in the works of healing, the miraculous power
was only the tool for the divine program.

The personal contacts with Jesus were convincing. Allowing
for the fact that resurrection of the body seemed to many theo-
retically irrational, and actually impossible in the case of Jesus,
it is surprising that so few of the disciples refused the direct
evidence or doubted the validity of their own senses. Some, like
Thomas, were initially unwilling to concede the reality, and
others were hesitant even after they saw Jesus, but nearly all
ultimately accepted the fact that He had risen.

The variety of times at which Jesus appeared supports the
truthfulness of the narratives. Mary Magdalene met the Master
in broad daylight, probably in the middle of the forenoon.
Cleopas and his companion walked with Him to Emmaus during
an afternoon, with supper about five o'clock. The catch of fish
on the lake of Galilee occurred shortly after dawn, with breakfast on the beach. Paul was intercepted by the heavenly voice
at high noon. The appearances were not séances held in darkened
rooms behind screens, where illusion or fraud could be perpe-
trated.

There can, therefore, be no reasonable doubt of the objective
reality of the evidence. If the Jesus of history actually lived, if
He spoke the teachings attributed to Him, and if He performed
the works with which He is credited, there is no inherent intellectual hindrance to believing that He lives again. Without
using extravagant language or unnatural statements the Gospel
writers and Paul acknowledge the resurrection to be miraculous,
but as natural to Jesus as walking is to the ordinary man. They
take for granted that He rose from the dead because it was the
logical and normal prerogative of the Son of God.

The Historical Results

The initial shock of Jesus' rejection by priests and people, the
disappointment occasioned by the collapse of plans for a king-

dom, and the uncertainty of their personal prospects left the disciples completely bewildered and despondent. Nothing in their immediate circumstances would encourage them to believe that they could begin a successful religious movement, since death had apparently vitiated Jesus' promises. His followers realized that they had espoused a lost cause, and that the only procedure remaining to them was a quiet return to their homes and previous occupations.

Disunity threatened the continuance of the group. Their varied temperaments and conflicting ambitions could easily have destroyed their association within a short time had they chosen to perpetuate it. Peter's brusqueness, John's hasty temper, Thomas' pessimism, and Philip's materialism would inevitably clash, and would tend to shatter an artificial unity. Jesus Himself recognized this danger when He urged them in His parting words to "love one another" (John 15:12). He knew that the impending catastrophe would scatter them and that only a force transcending their differences could avail to bind them together.

The Transformation of the Disciples

Between the crucifixion and the day of Pentecost a remarkable transformation took place, involving a complete reversal of the disciples' attitudes. The eleven men, huddled in an obscure upper chamber in Jerusalem "for fear of the Jews" (John 20:19), became the active nucleus of a group that openly defied the Sanhedrin and boldly accused it of crucifying its own Messiah. The imprisonment of their leaders and the rejection by the public did not deter them from publishing their testimony in every quarter of the city. They were heedless of opposition and dedicated themselves unreservedly to proclaiming the messiahship of Jesus.

Individual character was suddenly altered. Simon Peter had followed Jesus with an enthusiastic though blundering loyalty. He had openly confessed Him as the Son of God (Matt. 16:16), had vowed that he would never forsake his Master (John 13:37), and had bravely drawn a sword in Jesus' defense against the guard that arrested Him. After the capture in Gethsemane Peter followed to the house of Caiaphas, evidently intending to support Jesus at the ensuing trial. He failed to fulfill his intentions, for he repudiated any connection with the Lord and finally denied Him with an oath.

The psychological consequence of Peter's failure was a violent emotional reaction. Appalled by his own deed, which could never be retracted, he despaired of obtaining forgiveness. Another interview with Jesus was precluded by the swift succession of the trial and crucifixion. Peter had lost the joy of fellowship and his chief motive for living.

Notwithstanding the dismal failure to maintain his promised loyalty, Peter was completely different a few weeks later on the day of Pentecost. With amazing poise and courage he openly accused the Jewish rulers of having crucified their Messiah, and affirmed that God had restored Him to life. His speech was not merely a rash burst of enthusiasm, for he consistently persevered in his conviction and was ready to suffer persecution. The only adequate explanation for Peter's sudden change was the new viewpoint that the resurrection afforded.

Similar transformations occurred in other disciples. The cynical unbelief of Jesus' brethren (7:5) gave way before the convincing proof that Jesus had arisen, for James later became the leader of the church in Jerusalem. Thomas' sudden transition from skepticism to worship must have been produced by a powerful impulse, for it was contrary to the entire current of his previous mental habit. He did not even accept Jesus' invitation to touch the wounds and thus satisfy his desire for sensory evidence, but turned immediately from argument to adoration.

The most spectacular instance in the Biblical record occurred in the life of Saul of Tarsus. Like his fellow Pharisees he believed in the principle of resurrection (Acts 23:6, 8), but to him Jesus of Nazareth was an impostor who deserved the penalty of death. He undoubtedly had heard rumors that Jesus had risen, but did not credit them. Positive that Christianity was a pernicious heresy, he devoted himself to the task of exterminating it. His fanatical zeal took him to Damascus for the avowed purpose of bringing the believers to court for trial, but he never completed his errand. The manifestation of the risen Lord whom he encountered on the road changed him into a protagonist of the message that he had endeavored to suppress. The reversal of his actions, attitudes, and theology was so drastic that his contemporaries could scarcely believe it (9:21), and accepted his new profession only with hesitancy. He remarked later about the altered values of his life, "What things were gain to me, these have I counted loss for Christ" (Phil. 3:7).

The transformation of these personalities is indisputable, for they have left a permanent heritage of faith to the Christian church. There was nothing in their previous experience or attitudes to account for the change; in fact, without the resurrection the disciples of Jesus would probably have disbanded, and the world might never have heard of Him through their agency. They had no analogy by which to create the illusion of a resurrection, nor had they the singleness of purpose and the cohesion to launch a crusade. The difference, however, was not due to a gradual recovery from disappointment, nor was it the result of shifting cultural influences. The renewed faith and enthusiasm which these persons exhibited can only be attributed to the truth that Christ had risen and had imparted to them new life.

The Descent of the Holy Spirit

The descent of the Holy Spirit on the day of Pentecost was a second major result of the resurrection. Prior to the coming of Christ He had been active in restraining moral evil (Gen. 6:3). Under the dispensation of law He was the source of prophetic inspiration (I Sam. 10:5, 6) and of power (16:13), but He did not indwell the nation Israel as a whole. The promise of Joel, "I will pour out my spirit upon all flesh; and your sons and your daughters shall prophesy" (Joel 2:28), predicted an enduement exceeding that which the prophet had witnessed in his own era.

The promise of the Old Testament was renewed by Christ in His discourse to the Jews in Jerusalem at the Feast of Tabernacles. "On the last day, the great day of the feast, Jesus stood and cried, saying, If any man thirst, let him come unto me and drink. He that believeth on me, as the scripture hath said, from within him shall flow rivers of living water. But this spake he of the Spirit, which they that believed on him were to receive: for the Spirit was not yet given; because Jesus was not yet glorified" (John 7:37-39). John's explanatory footnote written subsequent to Pentecost states that the believers in Christ would receive the gift of the Spirit, but that this enduement was not immediately available because "Jesus was not yet glorified." In Johannine phraseology, "glorified" referred to the Passion, for Jesus said to the eleven disciples when Judas left their company, "Now is the Son of man glorified" (13:31). The same word is used in John 17:1 concerning the victorious conclusion of His mission. Jesus taught that the advent of the Spirit was contingent upon His ascension to the Father, and the ascension was dependent upon the resurrection.

For this reason the outpouring of the Spirit was proof positive that the Lord had risen. When He descended upon the disciples at Pentecost, in visible and audible manner, He introduced a new epoch in God's dealing with mankind. Peter, in his sermon at Pentecost, explained, "This Jesus did God raise up, whereof we all are witnesses. Being therefore by the right hand of God exalted, and having received of the Father the promise of the Holy Spirit, he hath poured forth this, which ye see and hear" (Acts 2:32-33). The truth which Peter declared became the cardinal tenet of the new faith, and its subsequent history is a corroboration of Christ's resurrection.

The Church

The growth of the church cannot be attributed solely to the uniqueness of its teaching. Many of its basic beliefs were inherited from Judaism, which was already well known. Some of its practices were sufficiently similar to those of other religions to obscure the fundamental differences existing between it and heathenism. To the casual observer the gospel of Christ might appear to be only one more Eastern cult, centered around some minor Messiah and shrouded in mysticism. The pagan public probably classed it with the mystery religions which were popular in the empire during the first century.

The Jewish heritage was not wholly advantageous, for it linked Christianity with a displaced and dispersed people. Although the wide distribution of synagogues afforded platforms from which the first preachers could proclaim the true Messiah, the record of Acts shows that they were quite uniformly repudiated by Judaism, and that the synagogues ultimately became their adversaries rather than their supporters. Furthermore, with rare exceptions, the advancing evangelism turned increasingly to the Gentiles, who were hesitant to accept any teaching or influence from the Jews. Christianity's Jewish origin would be as much of a hindrance to its progress as an aid.

Misunderstanding of the nature of the gospel and of the intentions of Christians evoked persecution. They were accused of being atheists because they did not worship any visible god, and of being antisocial because of their reaction against the immoral practices and amusements of their day. The necessity of meeting for worship in private houses after the normal hours of work created the appearance of furtiveness and secrecy, which immediately aroused suspicion concerning their motives. They were charged with various kinds of debauchery, and imperfect understanding of the nature of the Lord's Supper led to rumors of ceremonial murder and cannibalism.

Another obstacle for the church to overcome was its own divisiveness. Inevitably there were differences of opinion within its ranks over the interpretation of Scripture and the formulation of doctrine. Alien religious influences combining with some aspects of Christian doctrine spawned heresies and cults claiming the Christian name, but possessing little of its reality. As good coinage suffers depreciation when counterfeited, the church was corrupted by perverse sects, many of which ultimately disappeared.

Unlike other religions, Christianity was not supported by any national culture. Judaism survived the destruction of the independent commonwealth because the Jews retained it as the sole inalienable possession that could preserve their national character. The religions of the Greeks and of the Romans, of the Celts and of the Teutons were integral to the corporate life of their respective peoples and were sustained by pride in state or tribal worship. In contrast, the church from its inception was not attached to any ethnic group. It could claim no connection with patriotism; it was rather despised as antisocial and subversive. During the first three centuries it depended upon the tolerance of the rulers for its survival. Why should it have endured when the cults of Isis, Serapis, Mithra, and other non-ethnic religions perished so completely that their names are now known only to scholars?

Both for its origin and for its survival the church is dependent upon the fact of the resurrection. The conviction of this verity inspired the apostles to proclaim the unique message that God had given to the world a new revelation of His power in the person of Jesus Christ. Faith in Him became the distinguishing mark of the new community, and His personal superintendence of their progress thwarted the schemes of their enemies and opened new doors for their ministry. The constant sense of His living presence rendered the believers impervious to opposition and persistent in witnessing.

After making allowance for all natural causes such as the unique promise of eternal life, the futility of the pagan philosophies, the influence of political patronage, and a growing popular sympathy for a persecuted minority, the rise and growth of the church cannot be adequately explained apart from the resurrection. Maurice Goguel, one of the leading Continental authorities on ecclesiastical history, who does not acknowledge a literal physical return of Christ from death, writes, "The creative source of Christianity was the faith in the risen and glorified Jesus."[7] Although Goguel distinguishes between resurrection fact, which he denies, and the resurrection faith, which he allows, he admits that the faith was essential to Christianity.

In a recent work on *The Protestant Faith*, George Forell says:

[7] M. Goguel, *The Birth of Christianity*, translated from the French by H. C. Snape (New York: The Macmillan Company, 1954) , p. 29.

"It is the faith in the resurrection of Christ which explains the existence of the Christian church. Without this faith the Christian church would never have come into being, and should it ever lose this faith it will not last very long. The resurrection and the message of Christ are mutually interdependent. The resurrection is God's confirmation of the Gospel. That is why the apostle Paul says: 'If Christ hath not been raised, your faith is futile and you are still in your sins.' "[8]

These quotations, which could be paralleled from numerous other sources of widely differing viewpoints, agree that faith in the resurrection of Christ is the secret of the church's origin. United by a common conviction that Jesus was not dead but living, the disciples proceeded to proclaim His victory and to win others to their cause. The novelty of this conviction, the assurance of personal security, and its satisfying sequel to the promises and covenants of the Old Testament afforded the basis for a new movement and for a coherent theology that created the church.

Faith in a concept, however, is not a satisfactory explanation of the existence of the church, unless that concept was based on an event. Neither Jewish theology nor Gentile philosophy was predisposed to elevate the crucified prophet of Nazareth to the plane of messiahship or deity. In spite of His wise teaching and His indisputable miracles His death as a criminal permanently discredited Him in the eyes of His own nation. Rabbinic literature either ignored or repudiated Him, and only within comparatively recent time has Judaism been willing to acknowledge that Jesus made any contribution to its history.

The Gentile attitude was equally skeptical. How could a helpless victim of Jewish spite and of Roman cruelty accomplish the salvation of men? If He could not overcome His enemies, could He deliver anyone else? To the pagan philosophers such a concept would be ridiculous. If Jesus did not rise from the dead, there would be no reason for ascribing to Him a rank higher than any of the philosophers who purveyed their wisdom

---

[8] George W. Forell, *The Protestant Faith* (Englewood Cliffs, N. J.: Prentice-Hall, Inc., 1960), pp. 177-178.

in the market place and imparted it to their coteries of disciples. Since "the Easter faith" did not accord with Jewish Messianism or with Gentile philosophy, who invented it? There was no external stimulus in the intellectual world of the first century to produce such a doctrine. Although the concept of a bodily resurrection existed in Pharisaism, it was connected with the remote events of the last day, and not with any contemporary individual.

Only the Easter fact can provide an adequate cause for the Easter faith. Unless the historic Person to whom the disciples had given their initial allegiance actually returned to life and made contact with them, their belief had no rational origin. No abstract process of reasoning would have inspired them to create the message of the gospel, or to preach it persistently and boldly.

The development of the church in the first century confirmed the claims that Jesus had risen. The events chronicled in the book of Acts illustrate this principle clearly, for at each crisis the risen Christ intervened. He instituted the enterprise by sending the Holy Spirit on the day of Pentecost (Acts 2:33). The appearance to Stephen (7:55) endorsed the message which marked the beginning of the separation between Judaism and Christianity. The arrest of Paul on the road to Damascus secured a leader who inaugurated the missionary movement toward the Gentiles and who shaped the development of the church's theology (22:6-15). At the culmination of his career, the Lord's direct word encouraged him to proceed to Rome (23:11). Although few of these episodes are direct appearances, the narrative assumes active participation by Christ in every phase of the church's life.

The resurrection was indisputably the core of the church's faith and the main cause of its inception, affecting every aspect of its theological and ecclesiastical progress. Not only did this concept permeate the teaching of the New Testament; it also influenced the practices of the church in the post-apostolic period.

An outstanding effect of this influence is the Christian observance of worship on the first day of the week rather than on the Sabbath, which was kept tenaciously by all orthodox Jews. Since the first Christian converts came from Judaism, retaining its Scripture and much of its theology, it is unlikely that they would instantly discard all of its customs. Peter and John continued to worship in the Temple at Jerusalem after the day of Pentecost (3:1), and Paul preached in synagogues on the Sabbath during his Asiatic mission (13:14-16, 44; 16:13; 17:1, 2; 18:4). The natural tendency would have been to perpetuate the Sabbath as the day for Christian worship. The opposite was true, however, for Christians worshiped on the first day of the week.

A hint of this change appears in the account of Paul's visit to Troas, where he preached to the assembled Christians "upon the first day of the week" (20:7) when they gathered together to break bread. The text implies that the first day rather than the seventh was the regular time for meeting, which would mean that a transition from Jewish custom to Christian observance had already occurred.

A further statement appears in the *Epistle of Barnabas.* "Ye perceive how He [God] speaks: Your present Sabbaths are not acceptable to Me, but that is which I have made, [namely this] when, giving rest to all things, I shall make a beginning of the eighth day, that is, a beginning of another world. Wherefore, also, we keep the eighth day with joyfulness, the day also on which Jesus rose again from the dead."[9]

Justin Martyr, probably a contemporary of Barnabas, added his confirmation of the practice. "But Sunday is the day on which we all hold our common assembly, because it is the first day on which God, having wrought a change in the darkness and matter, made the world; and Jesus Christ our Saviour on the same day rose from the dead. For he was crucified on the day before that of Saturn (Saturday); and on the day after that of Saturn, which is the day of the Sun, having appeared to his apostles and disciples, he taught them these things, which we have submitted to you also for your consideration."[10] In spite of the fact that ritual tends to become static, the Christian church changed its

---

[9] *Epistle of Barnabas* XV.
[10] Justin Martyr, *Apology* I, lxvii.

day of worship to the first day of the week, in honor of the risen Lord.

Inasmuch as the earliest witnesses attribute the remarkable social and theological dynamic of Christianity to the resurrection, one cannot consistently affirm the effects and deny the cause, unless he can show that some other cause is equally capable of producing the same results. The change of religious and social mores, and the creation of a body of people characterized by a distinctive ethic and possessing a new dynamic, can best be explained by accepting the testimony of the New Testament.

VII   The Theology
of the Resurrection

The intrusion of so strange an event as the resurrection into
the customarily regular order of nature demands an explanation.
Any deviation from uniformity in a living complex is significant
when it can easily be explained, and doubly so when no rational
cause can be found for it. The normal trend of the universe is
from complexity to simplicity, from diversity to monotony, from
order to chaos. Death is the state of equilibrium into which life
lapses. A reversal of the process presupposes the intervention
of a power great enough to arrest decay and to inject a new
creative principle into the world.

Such a power can be explained only by acknowledging the
existence of deity. God is inescapable for anyone who has
endeavored to comprehend in one reasoned system the varied
complex of ideas, forces, and objects that compose the universe.

God, however, is not discoverable by any ordinary means of
scientific investigation. The telescope does not reveal His location
in space; the spectroscope does not detect any light rays that
are peculiar to deity; and the microscope does not disclose any
substance invisible to the naked eye that possesses His attributes.
God is not a compound to be analyzed chemically, nor is He a
physical law to be determined by experimentation. He cannot be
weighed, measured, or photographed. His being eludes the usual

tests for reality, yet without Him the universe has neither meaning nor purpose, and its organization is a greater puzzle than if His existence is predicated.

The failure to discover God by ordinary means of research is caused by the inadequacy of the instruments employed. The dissecting knife and the microscope of the biologist can reveal many facts about the substance and organization of man's anatomy but they cannot afford the slightest clue to his temperament and attitude. His thought processes and purpose of life can be apprehended only by observing him in action, which presupposes contact with a living being through conscious communication, not simply a laboratory experiment on an inert specimen. If God exists, man can realize His person only as He freely chooses to convey His mind and purpose through agencies of His own selection.

Such media of communication must be adequate to carry the content and meaning of the divine revelation and must express its message in comprehensible terms. Like an alphabet, which requires a sufficient number of symbols to represent the sounds of the language it conveys, the media should be familiar to those for whom the message is intended. The only medium that can transmit the knowledge of God to man is personality, for purely mechanical means cannot fully communicate one personality to another. The print in this book may impart the meaning of the author's thought, but it cannot convey the tone of voice or the feeling that the living presence would give to the reader.

The Resurrection and the Nature of God

God's revelation is transmitted by His Word (Greek: *Logos*) which embodies His thought and expression in human terms. As the Gospel of John states, "In the beginning was the Word [an external revelation], and the Word was with God [an approved revelation], and the Word was God [an adequate revelation]. . . . And the Word became flesh, and dwelt among us, and we beheld his glory [an understandable revelation]" (John 1:1, 14). Christ, the eternal Word, is the vehicle of revelation because He embodies in personality the nature and message of God for man.

The communication through Christ brought the revelation of God into the totality of human experience. He did not speak of only one aspect of God's character, nor solely on one occasion, but represented God's person in every situation of human life. "In him was life," the fullness of the divine vitality, "and the life was the light of men," the application of that vitality to all phases of human existence (1:4). The completeness of this revelation manifests itself in the most adverse circumstances, as the perfection of a flower is best viewed against the background of a ruined wall, or like a sweet strain of music remembered longest when it pierces the rumble of gunfire or the wailing of mourners.

This totality of experience includes the mysterious and tragic episode of death, the common fate of all men, who irrespective of social station, mental capacity, or physical strength ultimately pass to the grave. Death is the point at which even the semblance of certainty ends; for while life is unpredictable, death is a sealed book. If the revelation of God is inadequate, the real problem of human destiny will remain forever insoluble.

The revelation of the Word must therefore include the experience of death to demonstrate how God can grapple with it and remove its terrors. Only in this way can salvation be achieved; the Son of God must by tasting death for every man bring the fullness of God's resources to the rescue of human frailty. God's nature is disclosed chiefly through the redemptive process because the salvation of men is His most compelling motive for revealing Himself intimately. The revelation in creation exhibits His power and godhead through the magnificence of His works. The order and intricacy of nature, whether in the vast galaxies of space or in the ultramicroscopic structure of the atom, bespeak a designer of infinite intelligence and power. The processes of the created world may also intimate His providence and general goodness. The heart of God is manifested by His answer to the crisis confronting humanity in spiritual disaster and death. If God responds to this problem by the exercise of His omnipotence, His reaction will constitute the best possible key to His true nature.

The tension between the living God and death may be protracted, but its resolution comes in the moment when God acts decisively. Such an act need not be repeated, for a single occurrence is enough to prove God's disposition and ability to save. Furthermore, God's act must take place within the framework of recorded history if men are to build upon His intervention the reality of a secure hope. The logical conclusion of an a priori argument may be sound in its reasoning, but the abstract principles on which it is founded are never so convincing as an act which embodies the truth related to existing need. The resurrection of Christ is such an event, and is so characterized in the Scriptures.

Paul's prayer in Ephesians 1, which concentrates into a few words the meditation and experience of a lifetime, describes the redemptive character of God by the resurrection.

For this cause I also . . . cease not to give thanks for you, making mention of you in my prayers; that the God of our Lord Jesus Christ, the Father of glory, may give unto you a spirit of wisdom and revelation in the knowledge of him; having the eyes of your heart enlightened, that ye may know what is the hope of his calling, what the riches of the glory of his inheritance in the saints, and what the exceeding greatness of his power to us-ward who believe, according to that working of the strength of his might which he wrought in Christ, when he raised him from the dead, and made him to sit at his right hand in the heavenly places . . . (Eph. 1:15-20).

The epistle to the Ephesian Christians was designed to explain the implications of the gospel to a church that was beginning to be self-conscious theologically and to ponder upon the meaning of the revelation that had been vouchsafed to it. Contrasting sharply with the heathen concepts in which the members of the church had been nurtured, the gospel provided an entirely new characterization of God. Paul prayed that the Ephesians might realize its significance, expressed in the *hope* that God offered, the *glory* that believers could attain, and the *power* which He could impart. These qualities, said Paul, were exemplified in the resurrection of Christ.

"The *hope* of his calling" depicts the purposefulness of God. He plans the cosmic process to eventuate in victory for righteousness in spite of the prevalence of evil. To those who receive His revelation He gives the prospect of sharing in that victory when they shall have discharged the responsibilities that He has laid upon them. By this knowledge of God's purposeful action, life is liberated from overshadowing futility and despair. By raising Jesus from the dead God proved that human existence need not end in the tragedy of death.

God is, therefore, an active factor in the historical existence of man. By the resurrection of Christ the ceaseless cycle of birth and death is broken. The monotonous uniformity of the cosmos cannot become an imprisoning process, endless and devoid of progress or meaning. God has reversed the trend to oblivion and has shown that decadence is not a true reflection of His being. The resurrection is a flash of eternity in the darkness of time that illuminates, if only briefly, the real outline of God's personality.

"The glory of his inheritance in the saints" speaks of the pleasure that God derives from His redemptive work. The impartation of life to men who were "dead through . . . trespasses and sins" (Eph. 2:1), and the culmination of that life in a new society related to God and devoted to Him, creates an "inheritance" peculiarly His. The church will stand as an abiding memorial to the divine triumph over the corrosion of sin, and is a significant exception to the reign of death.

Insofar as the resurrection of Christ foreshadows the destiny of believers, it exhibits the delight of God in the effectiveness of His salvation and reflects His personal interest in the development of individuals and in the growth of the church as a whole. In accordance with the pattern set by Christ men will reach the highest potentialities that God has designed for them. Through the transformation of their character they become the perfected products of grace, a collective manifestation of God's creative and redemptive power. Just as an artist's paintings constitute an "inheritance" that witnesses to his vision, technique, and ability, so the varied personalities transformed by the resurrection life are the eternal exhibit of God's artistry in the church. Paul caught this concept when he said, "For we are his workmanship [*poema,* 'poems'], created in Christ Jesus for good works, which God afore prepared that we should walk in them" (Eph. 2:10).

The resurrection is the fullest disclosure of God's power to man because it has overcome his greatest obstacle. The perfection of life is frustrated by the presence of death, for when man attains the maturity and strength that would enable him to accomplish his finest work, decay and death overtake him. Rarely does anyone retain to old age sufficient vigor to execute the plans conceived in youth. The resurrection is the antithesis of human weakness, for it concentrates in one act the vastness of the divine strength. All four words for power commonly used in the New Testament (*dunamis,* reserve power; *energeia,* applied power; *kratos,* mastery or control; *ischus,* physical strength) are employed by Paul to describe the magnitude of God's resources employed in raising Christ from the grave. *Dunamis* is latent power, such as resides in water impounded by a dam or in the electrical charge in a battery. God is the great potential of the universe, the fount of all energy from which the processes of time and space derive their initial and continuing impulse. This potential lifts man out of the dominion of death and sets him on a new plane of hope. *Energeia* is the applied power that enables him, having once been released from the fear and hopelessness of death, to manifest the vitality of a new life. *Kratos* is the mastery of power, which energizes the human vehicle as the electric current activates a motor or lights a bulb by permeating the inert metal with its force. *Ischus* usually denotes physical strength, or the endowment of power constituting the vigor that any individual utilizes in work. The resurrection is the proof of God's omnipotence, for it demonstrates that His nature is power, and that He can re-create a world paralyzed by sin and devastated by death. Life is the natural expression of His being, neutralizing and reversing the law of entropy, by which the forces of the world ultimately subside into complete stagnation. God is mobile, active, creative, constantly intervening to arrest the trend to death, and vigorously assertive of His presence.

Our knowledge of the fatherhood of God is enriched by the resurrection. Paul, in characterizing God for the Galatian Christians, whose first concepts of deity had been drawn from their pagan training, spoke of Him as "God the Father, who raised him [Jesus] from the dead" (Gal. 1:1). Ancient literature called Zeus "the father of gods and men,"[1] but the term "father" meant "progenitor" rather than a guardian. The pagan gods were believed to be immortal, but they cared nothing for men, except, perhaps, a few favorites. The pagan view of the fatherhood of God implied only an antecedent existence, genetic origin, or superiority on the part of a god remote from men and only casually interested in them. The Christian concept is a picture of sacrificial love and of active intervention on behalf of those doomed to death. God through Christ has brought into the circle of His family those who had been alienated from Him, and He has made available a new source of life through the living Christ.

The resurrection speaks of the eternity of God. Death belongs to time, for as part of time's decay extended to man it limits him to the three-score years and ten of which the Scriptures speak (Ps. 90:10), and terminates his activities. Death is a constant reminder of the transient frailty of existence. By contrast, "Christ being raised from the dead dieth no more; death no more hath dominion over him" (Rom. 6:9). Christ, the image of God, is eternal and therefore the God whom He represents must be eternal.

The resurrection is the inevitable reaction of God's eternal nature when brought into contact with the decadence of time, rather than a single miraculous act performed to meet a crisis. As the ocean tides fill an empty harbor or as an electrical charge will set the idle motors of a factory in motion, so the power of God reanimates the deadness of the world. Christ's return from death is an abiding witness to a living God, who intervenes in His created order when necessity demands drastic action.

Acceptance of the witness of the resurrection is saving faith, the true foundation of spiritual life. To define faith Paul used the example of Abraham, whose bold trust in God made him the spiritual ancestor of all believers (Rom. 4:16). Perplexed by the

---

[1] *Iliad*, I, 544.

promise of a child when such an event seemed a biological impossibility (Gen. 17:15-17), and later by the dilemma of sacrificing the son on whom the fulfillment of his hopes depended (22:2), Abraham placed unswerving faith in "[the] God, who giveth life to the dead, and calleth the things that are not, as though they were" (Rom. 4:17). His faith became the standard for his successors. Paul asseverated that God was still able to fulfill His promises, for the Scripture "was not written for his [Abraham's] sake alone, . . . but for our sake also, unto whom it shall be reckoned, who believe on him that raised Jesus our Lord from the dead . . ." (4:23, 24).

A similar expression of confidence occurs in Paul's rehearsal of his physical hardships in Asia. Some misfortune, whether illness or persecution, overtook him while preaching in Ephesus. He wrote the Corinthian church that he was crushed by its pressure, so that his very life was endangered; he felt that a sentence of death had been passed on him (II Cor. 1:8-10). In spite of the menacing circumstances he put full trust in "God who raiseth the dead," and because of the outcome of this experience he exulted over God's past deliverance and guarantee of future protection.

Peter used the same phrase, "God, that raised him [Christ] from the dead" (I Pet. 1:21), in writing to Christians who were threatened with persecution. He reminded them that in spite of "manifold trials" (1:6) they possessed the assurance of God's mercy and power.

The resurrection, then, is the supreme declaration of God's true being. By this single act He has announced His purpose, His power, and His attitude toward man. Scripture records numerous events of great spiritual significance, but none other attests so completely or so convincingly the being of a living God.

The Resurrection and Salvation

The various creeds of Christendom, following the lead of the New Testament writers, have incorporated the resurrection among the distinctive doctrines of the faith. The Apostles' Creed, reputedly the oldest, includes it in summarizing the life of Christ, "he suffered under Pontius Pilate, was crucified, dead, and buried. The third day he arose from the dead . . . ." A second reference marks the conclusion, "I believe . . . in the resurrection of the dead and the life everlasting."

Neither this nor any of the more recent codes of Christian faith deals adequately with the connection of resurrection and salvation. Belief in the historical fact may be affirmed, but its relevance to one's personal relationship with God is ignored. By contrast, the Scriptures are explicit, for they treat the resurrection as a power to be applied as well as a fact to be acknowledged.

The figure of rising from the dead is a peculiarly fitting emblem of the regenerative process by which God reclaims sinners. Paul, speaking of the future salvation of Israel, says, "For if the casting away of them is the reconciling of the world, what shall the receiving of them be, but life from the dead?" (Rom. 11:15). The same imagery describes the present state of Gentile Christians who were "dead through . . . trespasses and sins" (Eph. 2:1), but have been "raised . . . up with him, and made . . . to sit with him in the heavenly places, in Christ Jesus" (2:6). In both instances the metaphor describing salvation is drawn from the historic event; it is not an artificial product of imagination.

Christ's glorious victory marks His death with unusual significance. Jesus was not the only one who died for His ideals or sacrificed Himself for His friends. Socrates was falsely accused of corrupting Athenian youth and sentenced to death by his judge. Refusing to escape, he drank without protest the poisonous hemlock administered by the jailer. In spite of the obvious miscarriage of justice, he maintained unswerving loyalty to the principles by which the Athenian state was governed. The readiness to forfeit life rather than to abandon principles places Socrates among the moral leaders of antiquity, but his death did not differ in character and finality from that of his contemporaries and could not remove the sins of the Athenians. At best it was only a prime example of calm fortitude and heroic courage.

Jesus insisted that His death had more than exemplary significance; it was redemptive. "The Son of man came not to be ministered unto, but to minister, and to give his life a ransom in exchange for many" (Mark 10:45; original translation). To a reader of the first century the term "ransom" always meant the price for the manumission of slaves. Even though these words may not have conveyed to Jesus' hearers the full implications of an organized soteriology, they predicated a voluntary substitution of Himself in the place of others in order that they might receive freedom and blessing.

In the discourse which precedes the above quotation, Jesus had discussed His approaching death and had inquired whether or not the disciples could drink the "cup" which He must drink or participate in the "baptism" which awaited Him. The impending crisis weighed upon Him heavily, for the humiliation of the cross would involve an apparent frustration of His designs and hopes, inexplicable to the disciples and to the world. The suffering would be almost unendurable and would inflict grief on all those related to Him. Why should He choose deliberately to accept this fate if it were a purposeless calamity? Obviously He regarded the apparent failure as a necessary step in the accomplishment of His mission and expected that the suffering of the cross would be validated by His resurrection.

While the Gospels state the principle of vicarious death only incidentally,[2] the Epistles offer more explicit teaching. Paul, writing to the Galatian churches, stated that Christ gave Himself for our sins that He might free us from this present evil age (Gal. 1:4). He summarized the essence of the gospel for the Corinthian Christians by saying, "Christ died for our sins according to the scriptures; . . . he was buried; . . . he hath been raised on the third day according to the scriptures; and . . . he appeared . . ." (I Cor. 15:3-5). The apostle emphasized the theological significance of Christ's death, stating that He "who knew no sin he [God] made to be sin on our behalf; that we might become the righteousness of God in him" (II Cor. 5:21). Paul's last allusion virtually repeated Jesus' words by declaring that He gave Himself "a ransom for all" (I Tim. 2:6).

---

[2] Cf. *supra*, pp. 43, 45, 59, 85.

The Petrine writings substantiate this interpretation in almost identical language. "[He] bare our sins in his body upon the tree, that we, having died unto sins, might live unto righteousness" (I Pet. 2:24). "Christ also suffered for sins once for all, a righteous man in the place of unrighteous men, that He might lead us into the presence of God" (I Pet. 3:18, original translation).

The First Epistle of John affirms the same truth. Christ, the living advocate in the presence of God, is the "righteous one" whose blood is the propitiation for sins (I John 2:2; 4:10). Christ's sacrifice in past time is inextricably linked to the church's life in the present. The Apocalypse continues the same thought saying, "[He] loveth us, and loosed us from our sins by his blood" (Rev. 1:5). "Loveth," in the present tense, implies current and continuous action; "loosed," in the past tense, refers to an accomplished event.

In the major texts dealing with the doctrine of atonement for sin through the death of Christ, the resurrection is either expressed or implied. Sparrow-Simpson[3] raises the question whether it is simply an aid to faith, or whether it is the direct cause of justification. Since the death of Christ is the basis of forgiveness, does the resurrection possess more than the auxiliary value of corroborative evidence?

In alluding to the atonement the writers make clear that without continuing life the death would be ineffective. Not the inert sacrifice, but the sacrifice presented and applied by the living Lord is the assurance that the record of past sins has been erased and that forgiveness is available daily for spiritual aid. Christ, raised from the dead, died to sin once for all, and His present life is the pledge of a new relationship to God for those whom He has rescued (Rom. 8:34).

The pattern of thought outlined in the Pauline and Johannine writings is reinforced by the argument of the book of Hebrews. Following principles embodied in the sacrificial laws of the Old Testament, the author explained the death of Christ in

---

[3] W. J. Sparrow-Simpson, *The Resurrection and Modern Thought* (New York: Longmans, Green, and Company, 1911), p. 301.

terms of an offering. If, he reasoned, the blood of animals can avail to remove ceremonially the defilement of the flesh, the sacrifice of Christ can clear the burdened conscience of guilt and prepare believers to receive the heritage of God's blessings (Heb. 9:14, 15). The shedding of blood was necessary to the just forgiveness of sin.

The finality of this offering and its permanent efficacy are assured by the living presence of Christ before the Father. He need not repeat His sacrifice as the high priest annually re-enacted the ceremonial offerings on the Day of Atonement. "Now once [for all] at the end of the ages hath he been manifested to put away sin by the sacrifice of himself" (Heb. 9:26). No further offering is necessary, because His return to life is God's seal of approval which assures the perpetuation of its efficacy. "He, when he had offered one sacrifice for sins for ever, sat down on the right hand of God" (10:12). The resurrection thus unites the sacrifice and the priest into one person whose constant ministration assures the perpetuity of forgiveness of sin and of deliverance from death. It guarantees the competence of the Saviour to protect and to nurture those whom He has reconciled to God.

At the conclusion of Paul's great discourse on salvation in the first eight chapters of Romans, he deals with the future of the Christians. Will the atonement afford assurance that neither the unforeseen tests of life nor the rigors of final judgment can shake their confidence? To the rhetorical question "Who is he that condemneth?" Paul replies by another: "Shall Christ Jesus that died [condemn us], yea, rather, that was raised from the dead, who is at the right hand of God, who also is making intercession for us?" (Rom. 8:34, original translation). The performance of the believer is not dependent upon his resolution or righteousness in itself but is the result of the direct ministration and intercession of the unchanging Christ who has risen from the dead to make His salvation effectual.

By the continuing work of Christ the permanence of salvation is assured. Dogmas may become irrelevant when the setting to which they apply changes; arguments for a doctrinal position may become antiquated; experience may grow dim and meaningless;

but a living personality always exercises an impact on its environment and upon the other personalities with whom it interacts. The fact that Christ arose to fulfill His promises and to perfect His purpose prevents Christian theology from fading into the limbo of outworn myth. Its truth is unalterable because He is the same yesterday, today, and forever.

The resurrection is thus basic to the salvation of the entire body of believers. The corporate exercise and enjoyment of divine grace is as essential to spiritual development as the individual perfection of each believer. By association the members of this new body learn from each other, and support each other in Christian living. These mutual endeavors were never intended to be haphazard, for they were to be directed by the living Lord of the church. As the group expanded by multiplying adherents and by extending evangelistic activities, it depended increasingly on the guidance of the risen Head. The resurrection was a constant reality to the Christians because they were observing its effects in their daily growth.

When the church sought to reach others with the message of the gospel, it found that repentance and revival were the gifts of the living Christ (Acts 5:31). The martyrdom of Stephen, the most promising apologist of the infant community, seemed a harbinger of defeat and of possible extinction, but Christ intervened to receive Stephen to Himself (7:59). By the conversion of Saul of Tarsus He transformed the chief persecutor into a more potent evangelist than Stephen had been (9:20-22). He guided the apostles in numerous decisions of missionary policy, making their strategy effective in planting churches throughout the Roman world. The vision of the Apocalypse depicts Him as the protector of the churches, supporting their leaders by His right hand and walking among them to encourage or reprove as circumstances might necessitate (Rev. 1:17-20).

The church, therefore, is not completely autonomous, adjusting its theology and policies to shifting contemporary standards at its own discretion. Far from being mementoes of a bygone day which must be distorted from their original framework to fit the new age, the person and ethic of Christ are the expression of the

Lord, who is living and accessible. Insofar as He is unchanging, the historic revelation of His incarnation remains valid; to the extent that He interacts with the church, through the Holy Spirit, the message is new and fresh. As the church receives and obeys the message, it enjoys the fullness of corporate salvation.

The active principle in perfecting the individual believer is the resurrection of Christ. "It is no longer I that live, but Christ liveth in me," said Paul to the Galatians (2:20). The apostle Paul was not speaking only of adopting the ideals of Christ, but of definite control by the risen Lord (1:1). The entrance of Christ into one's life introduces reviving and renewing power.

Paul uses another figure to make plain his meaning. "Awake, thou that sleepest, and arise from the dead, and Christ shall shine upon thee" (Eph. 5:14), a fragment of an early Christian poem, is similar in thought. The unbeliever, "dead in trespasses and sins" (2:1 KJ), is brought to life by the power of Christ and is elevated to a state of victory. The victory, to be constant, must be maintained by the same power that produced it. If salvation applies only to ultimate release from the penalty of sin, and not to the present problem, it becomes meaningless for everyday emergencies.

The necessity for a constant internal moral dynamic to resist the attacks of temptation and to check natural impulses to evil was felt keenly by the apostolic writers. Undoubtedly they believed in a complete salvation through Christ, but how could it be realized? Their concept of salvation had broadened from the political reconstitution of Israel and from forgiveness of its national sins to an act of God including the Gentiles within its blessings. The formation of a body composed of both Jews and Gentiles, confronting the pagan world with a message of supernatural deliverance, demanded that a new kind of life be manifested. Convincing demonstration of this claim could be realized only through those who made it. The objective reality of salvation contingent upon Christ's triumph over death must be exemplified morally and spiritually by an analogous inward experience.

The parallel of Christian experience with the resurrection

begins with baptism. Paul discussed the incompatibility of sin and grace in his letter to the Christians in Rome.

Are ye ignorant that all we who were baptized into Christ Jesus were baptized into his death? We were buried therefore with him through baptism into death: that like as Christ was raised from the dead through the glory of the Father, so we also might walk in newness of life. For if we have become united with him in the likeness of his death, we shall be also in the likeness of his resurrection; knowing this, that our old man was crucified with him, that the body of sin might be done away, that so we should no longer be in bondage to sin; for he that hath died is justified from sin. But if we died with Christ, we believe that we shall also live with him; knowing that Christ being raised from the dead dieth no more; death no more hath dominion over him. For the death that he died, he died unto sin once: but the life that he liveth, he liveth unto God. Even so reckon ye also yourselves to be dead unto sin, but alive unto God in Christ Jesus (Rom. 6:3-11).

Paul takes for granted the initial confessional act of baptism, which was the normal gateway to a professed faith. The author's chief concern was not the possibility of forgiveness of sins, but continuation in a life of holiness. Since a believer has accepted the baptism which unites him with Christ in death, he is obligated to accept also the new kind of life which that death introduces. He can no longer rightfully engage in the practices that evoked God's wrath and that necessitated the cross. Only the negative aspect, however, is insufficient. If death marks the cessation of indulgence in evil, the resurrection is emblematic of positive righteousness, a life lived in harmony with God. Christ, having passed through death, has emerged into a glory which He desires to share with men. Sanctification is assent to the death that separates from sin, and appropriation of the vitality that empowers for righteousness.

By this practical analogy the resurrection becomes the pattern for spiritual life, embracing both the realism of human sin and struggle, and the idealism of the divine plan and purpose. The resultant theology affords an adequate integration of what exists and of what ought to be, for no other unites in historic action the ideal concepts of truth with the harsh realities of this world. Paul warned the Colossian Christians against permitting anyone to rob them of their faith by specious reasoning or by mystic wiles in accord with the prevailing cults of their day, since truth had been revealed to them in the person of Christ. In words which parallel Romans 6 he reminded them that they had been "buried with [Christ] in baptism" and "raised with him through faith in the working of God" (Col. 2:12). Because they had been representatively raised with Christ, he urged them to "seek the things that are above, where Christ is, seated on the right hand of God" (3:1).

The spiritual aspect is obviously figurative. The Christian remains for the present in a material body, without any change in its composition or location. Morally and spiritually he has been transformed and transferred to a different environment. His interests are centered in Christ, his perspective is now from the heavenly scene rather than from the earthly, and his criteria of ethical behavior are changed completely.

The numerous practical injunctions in the epistles are founded upon the historical fact. On the assumption that Christians have "risen" with Christ, Paul urged his readers to put to death all manifestations of evil such as "fornication, uncleanness, passion, evil desire, and covetousness, which is idolatry" (Col. 3:5). Such indulgences would be utterly incongruous with the new life. On the contrary, he commanded that Christians shall cultivate "a heart of compassion, kindness, lowliness, meekness, longsuffering" and a forgiving spirit (3:12, 13). In both positive and negative commands, the active verb is followed by "therefore," making it the logical sequel to the new spiritual vitality and position that Christ has imparted.

The Petrine teaching resembles Paul's closely. "[You] through him are believers in God, that raised him from the dead, and gave him glory; so that your faith and hope might be in God. . . . Putting away therefore all wickedness, and all guile, and hypocrisies, and envies, and all evil speakings, as newborn babes, long for the spiritual milk . . . , that ye may grow thereby unto salvation" (I Pet. 1:21; 2:1-2). Peter's introduction of the final clause by "therefore" corresponds to Paul's conclusion in Colossians that the new life established by revelation and redemption in Christ involves a higher standard of conduct for Christians. The interim between initial conversion and ultimate glorification is not a parenthesis but a progressive realization of the immediacy of the new life in Christ.

Within the scope of resurrection life lies also the provision for present physical needs. If the Lord Jesus Christ is as much alive today as when He walked on earth, He is still able to heal the sick and to strengthen the weak. His power is undiminished, and His good will has not been withdrawn.

The first miracle recorded in the book of Acts concerns a man who, because he was born with ankles that would not support his weight, was doomed to a life of beggary. While he sat by the Beautiful Gate of the Temple waiting for some kindly person to fling him a coin, one day he saw Peter and John approaching. Awaiting their arrival, the lame man kept hoping for a generous donation. His disappointment at Peter's salutation, "Silver and gold have I none" (Acts 3:6), turned to amazement as the apostle continued, "What I have, that give I thee. In the name of Jesus Christ of Nazareth, walk." A new vitality surged through him, and jumping to his feet he began to run, and leap, and praise God.

To the queries of the crowd who wondered how this miracle had been effected, Peter replied: ". . . God raised [Christ] from the dead; whereof we are witnesses. And by faith in his name hath his name made this man strong, whom ye behold and know: yea, the faith which is through him hath given him this perfect soundness in the presence of you all" (3:15-16). The apostle ascribed the healing directly to faith in a risen Christ, whose response to faith had cured the beggar.

A hint that the same power can be applied to present physical need appears in Pauline teaching. "If the Spirit of him that raised up Jesus from the dead dwelleth in you, he that raised up Christ Jesus from the dead shall give life also to your mortal bodies through his spirit that dwelleth in you" (Rom. 8:11).

A well-attested variant of this text would alter the final words to read, ". . . because of his Spirit that dwelleth in you," which suggests that the Spirit's indwelling is the guarantee rather than the medium of resurrection power.[4] The crux of the interpretation lies in the words "mortal bodies," which mean literally "bodies subject to death." The adjective could scarcely be applied to a body already dead, for only a live body could be "subject" or "liable" to death. If, then, Paul refers to the living body, he declares that it can be refreshed or strengthened by the continuous impartation of the life of Christ. Immortality of the present body is never promised, but the power of the resurrection may be appropriated to meet the recurrent strain of daily activity. Since the Holy Spirit inhabits the body as His temple, He can be trusted to keep His dwelling in good repair as long as He needs it in His service.

Paul's epigram, "The body is . . . for the Lord; and the Lord for the body: and God both raised the Lord, and will raise up us through his power" (I Cor. 6:13-14), corroborates the teaching of Romans. Although the theme of I Corinthians does not relate primarily to physical health, the phrase "the Lord for the body" implies by reciprocation that if the body is devoted to God, He will be concerned for its welfare and will ultimately transform it by raising it from the dead. The Christian's well-being is a prelude to the resurrection, and is maintained by the same vital force that will ultimately recall him from death.

The Resurrection and Eschatology

The application of the resurrection to the believer involves a state not yet realized. Eschatology, which deals with events to come, is highly important because the future determines the value of the present. Adversities may be quickly forgotten if they are explained as the inevitable prelude to success; prosperity may become a haunting memory if it is followed by disaster. Only

---

[4] Greek: *dia to enoikoun autou pneuma*. The reading is supported by the following New Testament manuscripts: B, D, G, the old Latin and Syriac, and the majority of the Byzantine manuscripts.

the final outcome can show whether present events are truly good or evil in their ultimate effect, and only the judgment of God can be decisive.

For Christians the resurrection determines their final status. It is, therefore, pivotal in eschatological teaching and essential to a complete understanding of the process of redemption. Paul, defending his position before the Jewish Sanhedrin in the framework of the Old Testament revelation, said, "Brethren, I am a Pharisee, a son of Pharisees: touching the hope and resurrection of the dead I am called in question" (Acts 23:6). Although his allusion was admittedly a subterfuge to divide the council (24:21), he did not repudiate the truth of the statement. On the contrary, he re-emphasized it, affirming that he believed "all things which are according to the law, and which are written in the prophets; having hope toward God . . . that there shall be a resurrection both of the just and unjust" (24:14-15). Paul aligned himself with the Pharisees, who believed in ultimate bodily renewal, as the Sadducees did not (23:8), and thus he declared the continuity of the New Testament faith with the Old Testament revelation. In each of his epistles, from the salutation of the letter to the Galatians (1:1) to the farewell in II Timothy (2:8), Paul maintained an unbroken testimony to this consummation of God's redemptive action.

Apart from an objective, redemption is futile. Salvation ending in death or extinction would be no salvation at all, since God's greatest effort would be doomed to failure. The historical process of divine revelation which has disclosed God's power and purpose through the slow unfolding of the ages will inevitably be consummated in the defeat of sin and death. Such a consummation must be a definite event in time, for a true climax must terminate one action and inaugurate another. Just as Christ's resurrection took place on a given day in history, so the completion of God's plan for men will be an event as truly historical as Cornwallis' surrender at Yorktown.

Christian eschatology is the systematic definition of the future redemptive purpose to be accomplished in Christ. The church has always looked forward to the establishment of a new creation from which sin and death will be forever outlawed. Whether it be the broad initiation of the Messianic kingdom, or whether it be the particular destiny of an individual, the resurrection is equally involved. The last great act of God's saving grace will be the defeat and reversal of death.

This victory implies the raising of the body, for the reconstitution of man's natural being transcends mere survival of personality. Biblical revelation differs from the philosophical concept of immortality widely current among the thinkers of antiquity, many of whom believed in the immortality of the soul, but few of whom entertained the concept of a physical life beyond death. Paul was ridiculed at Athens for preaching that the dead could be raised. As soon as he announced that the power of Jesus to judge the world was confirmed by His resurrection, the audience politely informed him that they would hear him again at some other time, and quickly withdrew (Acts 17:32).

To the Greek philosophers perpetuation of corporeal existence was neither credible nor desirable. The body was a prison which hindered spiritual progress, an obstacle in the path to the knowledge of God. The idealism which they espoused regarded matter as the seat of evil. The highest good could be attained only through liberation from the appetites and drives of the body, and by finding freedom in pure spiritual being. In such a philosophy death would not be an enemy but a benefactor. If death is a release, there would be no advantage in returning to the limitations of flesh.

Life for the Christian is not an escape but a conquest. Corporeal limitations are not abolished by death but are overcome by new powers which the resurrection can confer. The body is not a hindrance to the spirit because it is material; it is rather an imperfect instrument which needs only a vitalizing touch to make it an acceptable medium for the expression of the highest life. Even with its present defects and weaknesses it is an intricate mechanism, so highly organized that no machine can equal its potential for usefulness or its adaptability to surroundings. It operates in the cold of the Antarctic and in the heat of the tropics; it can provide its own locomotion in water or on land; the cells of its nervous system are more numerous than the units of a telephone exchange and will respond more quickly to stimuli. As the Psalmist said, man is fearfully and wonderfully made. To abandon the body to decay would be defeat, the dereliction of men's material being. If salvation is the renewal of the whole person, the body is just as much a candidate for regeneration as the spirit.

Resurrection is the consummation of hope and the completion of redemption. The New Testament does not portray the future life as the ethereal survival of a disembodied ghost, nor is its viewpoint crassly materialistic. It resists exact definition because it is not analogous to any existing state and consequently cannot be expressed in ordinary terminology.

Perhaps the best way to understand this truth is to examine the metaphors used to describe it, such as the figure of the grain. Jesus said, "Except a grain of wheat fall into the earth and die, it abideth by itself alone; but if it die, it beareth much fruit" (John 12:24). Although He stressed the fruitfulness of sacrifice rather than the certainty of resurrection, the latter concept is latent in the words. The Pauline usage is plainer. "That which thou thyself sowest is not quickened, except it die: and that which thou sowest, thou sowest not the body that shall be, but a bare grain, it may chance of wheat, or of some other kind . . ." (I Cor. 15:36-37). The living plant that springs from the inert kernel is a renewal of life from death.

Continuity without exact similarity is also implied by this metaphor. The change from one body to another is not so radical that no connection between the two is discernible. Just as the plant cannot exist without the seed, there must be some persisting element that begins the new life. Even though the nature of the future body may be different from that of the present body, there must be some continuing link relating the one to the other and providing a basis for identification.

The paradoxical principle of concomitant change of appearance and identity of person is observable in the normal process of aging. In five years features and size may be so altered that recognition is difficult; nevertheless, the identity of the person persists. In similar fashion a restored body expressing the being of the same person who died will naturally bear the imprint of the personality even though the powers of the organism may be enhanced.

A second metaphor emphasizes the difference between the two bodies. "All flesh is not the same flesh; but there is one flesh of men, and another flesh of beasts, and another flesh of birds, and another of fishes" (I Cor. 15:39). Within the animate creation are various kinds of bodies which are tangible and visible, and which can make contact with each other. They are not identical in material, for the texture of chicken is not like that of beef, nor is beef like that of fish. The differences are not considered miraculous; they are normal features of nature. It is not incredible that God might produce another type of body which would be as different from man's as flesh from fowl, and which would yet be capable of maintaining human contacts. Just as birds and animals may exist in the same general environment and be adapted to different living conditions, so it may be possible for the resurrection body to inhabit the human plane of existence and to rise above it at will.

A third metaphor is taken from astronomy. "There is one glory of the sun, and another glory of the moon, and another glory of the stars; for one star differeth from another star in glory" (I Cor. 15:41). The observation was not made from the viewpoint of an astronomer, but by a man who had often watched the stars and planets wheel overhead as he traveled across the Mediterranean by boat, or along the Roman roads under the brilliant unclouded skies of the Middle East. He was impressed by the varying radiance of the heavenly bodies, some of which were so bright that they seemed like small suns, while others were mere pinpoints of light. As these differ in glory, so do the material body and the resurrection body. Perhaps Paul was thinking of the radiant Person who confronted him on the road to Damascus, blinding him with light and convincing him that the Jesus whom Stephen preached had really risen.

With these metaphors to aid description, the Biblical revelation predicates four characteristics of the resurrection body. First, it is *incorruptible*. Although the present body is a marvel of mechanical precision and intricacy, it is still subject to deterioration. Infection can reduce it to a putrid mass; disease can cripple or destroy it; and once life has gone from it, the body decays and disintegrates into dust. It may resist the attacks of time and tension for many years, but sooner or later its strength diminishes, the organs lose their elasticity and keenness of sense, and the entire mechanism collapses. At best it is a shabby housing for an eternal spirit.

There is no inherent reason why the body could not be immune to decay. The fact that the present corporeal structure can withstand disease and accident for seventy years, more or less, favors the possibility. The principle of resurrection makes this possibility an actuality. Removal of the tensions of guilt and doubt, and the impartation of a new divine energy will liberate men from the slow dissolution which is the inevitable consequence of sin. Eternal vigor is an accompaniment of the new life.

A second characteristic of the resurrection body is *glory*, contrasted with dishonor. The present physical body perishes in disgrace. Burial is necessary in order to prevent its decay from becoming nauseous and injurious to the public. In the famous gravedigging scene of Shakespeare's *Hamlet*,[5] the hero philosophized over a skull which one of the gravediggers had exhumed. It belonged to the court jester whom Hamlet had known in his childhood, and who had provided him with many a happy frolic. He held the skull in his hand long enough to say, "Alas, poor Yorick!" and then quickly cast it away in disgust because of its stench. The man who had been his playmate in bygone years had become a ghastly offense because of death. Mortality can end only in despair, but the resurrection body, freed from decay, will be radiant with the light of God. As the Transfiguration temporarily gave to the body of Jesus the glory of celestial life, so the final transformation of the Christian will occur when

---

[5] *Hamlet*, Act V, Scene 1.

Christ shall "fashion anew the body of our humiliation, that it may be conformed to the body of his glory, according to the working whereby he is able even to subject all things unto himself" (Phil. 3:21). The perfection of bodily health and the heightening of physical powers will be part of all believers' future physical heritage.

Power is another quality of the resurrection body, contrasted with present impotence. For its size the human body is surprisingly weak. If a man could carry in his hands a load as heavy in proportion to his weight as an ant can carry in its jaws, he would be able to handle half a ton. If he could jump like a grasshopper he could clear thirty feet in a single bound. A dog can detect sounds that the human ear never hears. Man has not the endurance of a bird, nor the muscle of a bear, nor the fleetness of an antelope. In physical abilities he is outstripped by almost every member of the animal creation.

Furthermore, man is susceptible to the invasion of the unseen enemies of disease and pestilences. Germs so tiny that they are invisible can ruin his physique and bring it down to the grave. A microbe that has neither consciousness nor intelligence can undermine vitality and destroy the intricate frame that has taken years to build. The natural body is weak and perishable, susceptible to every kind of illness and injury.

By contrast, the resurrection body will possess power. Speculation concerning its qualities is futile, since there is no definite scriptural statement defining its properties. Jesus seemed to have the ability to appear and disappear at will, to penetrate solid obstacles such as walls, and to exercise the ordinary bodily senses in a higher and sharper degree. He may well have exemplified the restoration of God's original design for man's physique, which would have been fulfilled had he progressed in obedience and righteousness. The first man had access to the "tree of life," the opposite of death, which was planted in Eden and was not withheld (Gen.2:9). Instead he chose the forbidden fruit of the tree of the knowledge of good and evil (3:6) and was consequently prevented from participating in the full benefit of everlasting life (3:22). Adam's disobedience severed him from God, the source of power, and gradually nullified the development of the faculties with which God had originally endowed him.

Paul drew a final contrast between the "natural" and the "spiritual" bodies. These words are the adjectives drawn from the nouns "soul" (*psyché*) and "spirit" (*pneuma*). "Soul" relates to the conscious life of animate beings. By creation man became a living soul, self-motivating and capable of communicating with other beings equal or inferior to himself. In this respect he is like the animals, whom he resembles in physiological structure and functions. The "natural" man lives on a purely animal level; he is dominated by his sensory and material desires. His outlook is bounded by the present. His philosophy is "Let us eat and drink, for to-morrow we die" (I Cor. 15:32). "Spirit" relates to the aspect of man's nature which can communicate with God. Unlike the animal, man has a capacity for worship and for fellowship with his Maker. The "spiritual" man receives the revelation of the Spirit of God and begins to understand the mind of God (2:11-16). As he matures under the direction of the Holy Spirit, he attains a new level of thought and conduct.

The present body, although it is marvelously organized, is incapable of expressing adequately the life of the spirit. In order that the redeemed and transformed spirit of man may have a proper channel for the expression of the new life, there must be an outward transformation corresponding to the inward change. The new understanding that accompanies fellowship with God requires a keener sensitivity to the whole of creation if the wonders of God's person and of His works are to be fully comprehended. Furthermore, a better instrument than the present body will be necessary for the eternal service which the redeemed man will offer to God.

The relation of mind and body is a mystery, but there is an undoubted interaction between the two. Glandular action and physical development or injury modify personality, and, conversely, mental and spiritual states affect the body. Lack of sleep produces tension and depression; worry may induce ulcers. Hereditary weakness may predispose some men toward one temptation, others toward another. Neither sin nor righteousness is a direct result of bodily states; they are the outcome of the will; but the defects of the present body may prove a handicap to spiritual and moral life.

The resurrection body will be a new instrument and dwelling for the redeemed spirit. Nowhere does the New Testament catalog its properties, but it does say, "we shall be like him; for we shall see him even as he is" (I John 3:2). Jesus' body was that of a man in the prime of life, fully matured and seasoned, and yet unaffected by the slow decline of middle age. He could transcend the ordinary physical limitations to which men are subject. Though He conformed to physical laws, He was not bound by them. His body was not subject to decay but was eternal in nature. As Adam was the progenitor of the human race, and transmitted by procreation the mechanism of the body which possessed derived life, so Christ is the head of the new race, which draws its life from Him and will ultimately feel the power of that life in physical transformation.

How can this transformation be effected when a body has completely dissolved into dust, and when its chemical components have been absorbed into other organisms?

What connection is there, if any, between the corpse that is laid in the grave and the body that shall be raised? At the raising of Jesus, decay had not commenced; the flesh and bones of the crucified body remained intact. The return to life was miraculous, but the materials had not disintegrated. The situation is different with the vast majority of His followers who have passed away during the last nineteen centuries.

When the body of Roger Williams, founder of the Rhode Island colony, was exhumed for reburial, it was found that the root of an apple tree had penetrated the head of the coffin and had followed down Williams' spine, dividing into a fork at the legs. The tree had absorbed the chemicals of the decaying body and had transmuted them into its wood and fruit. The apples, in turn, had been eaten by people, quite unconscious of the fact that they were indirectly taking into their systems part of the long-dead Williams. The objection may therefore be raised: How, out of the complex sequence of decay, absorption, and new formation, will it be possible to resurrect believers of past ages, and to reconstitute them as separate entities?

The answer to this quandary is contained in Paul's analogy of the seed. When a grain of wheat is dropped into the ground, its husk quickly decays, and even the live core disintegrates. The life of the seed, rather than its material substance, provides the continuity of existence. As the rootlets begin to grow, they draw nourishment from the earth, and by the chemistry of sun and rain the small seed soon becomes a large plant. The plant bears no external resemblance to the seed, nor is the bulk of its tissue drawn from the seed; nevertheless, the continuity is undeniable. There is persistence of type, because a given seed will always produce its own kind. Identity of type is not incompatible with discontinuity of substance.

Continuity of individuality is assured by the persistence of the personality, which God will reclothe with a body. Jesus' statement, "all that are in the tombs shall hear his voice, and shall come forth; they that have done good, unto the resurrection of life; and they that have done evil, unto the resurrection of judgment" (John 5:28-29), assumes the preservation of individuality, since those that have been buried will be restored to life. The restoration, however, is not a reconstitution of the original body that was interred, but a new structure patterned on the resurrection body of Christ. "As we have borne the image of the earthy, we shall also bear the image of the heavenly" (I Cor. 15:49).

If the foregoing concept seems to be based wholly on a biological model, not allowing for a "spiritual" or nonmaterial view of the resurrection, one should remember that the continuity of human personality does not depend upon matter. While speaking one night, the author noticed a stranger who seemed unusually attentive. He was totally unfamiliar, however, for the speaker could not identify him. After the service the stranger introduced himself, and he proved to be a classmate of thirty-five years before. A second look established unquestionable identity with the friend of past days, but the change was great enough to keep him from being recognized immediately. Many tissues of the body change completely every seven years, some more often, a few not at all. A man fifty years of age will have in his body only a fraction of the cells with which he began life; but despite the variations in appearance and material, the identity persists in continuity of consciousness and in the general form and habits of the body. If, then, in the resurrection there be continued memory of the past and a form that preserves recognizable characteristics in features and in movement, the fact of chemical and physical disintegration should be no obstacle to faith.

Although the present body is mortal and corruptible, and therefore temporary, the bodily state is not to be despised as inferior or shameful. God's redemption affects the total being— body, soul, and spirit. Since man is a unit, he cannot experience a complete salvation unless the body is affected as well as his spiritual nature. Full redemption involves being "clothed upon with our habitation which is from heaven" in order that life may be perfectly triumphant (II Cor. 5:2, 4). The fulfillment of creative purpose necessitates the manifestation of the divine glory in every aspect of human existence.

Although the foretaste of resurrection power is imparted to every believer through the Holy Spirit (II Cor. 5:5), the consummation has not yet occurred. Indeed, without the future event the present work of the Spirit would be meaningless, for His promises and ministry now are preparatory for a goal yet to be attained. Paul describes the tensions of the present life occasioned by the struggles of the created world against the corrupting elements of sin. He prophesies a coming manifestation of "the liberty of the glory of the children of God" (Rom. 8:21), adding, "And not only so, but ourselves also, who have the firstfruits of the Spirit, even we ourselves groan within ourselves, waiting for our adoption, to wit, the redemption of our body" (8:23).

Redemption of the body constitutes the outward evidence of completed salvation. Although the inward work of God's grace may be manifested through the behavior and expression of the present body, there is no fixed visible distinction between a believer and an unbeliever that can be discerned by a casual glance. The plan of God includes a transformation that will effect such a distinction, "the revealing of the sons of God" (8:19).

"Glory" is the term applied to the destiny of God's children. "Whom he justified," says Paul, "them he also glorified" (8:30). Jesus Himself implied this prospect when He declared that the righteous would "shine forth as the sun in the kingdom of their Father" (Matt. 13:43), sharing the likeness of the Lord whose "countenance was as the sun shineth in his strength" (Rev. 1:16). Acknowledged by God as His family, they will bear His image, not in a broken and marred form, but in the perfection of a new creation. All believers are now children of God through the new birth (John 1:12), but the full manifestation of that sonship awaits the revelation of Christ. "Beloved, now are we children of God, and it is not yet made manifest what we shall be. We know that, if he shall be manifested, we shall be like him; for we shall see him even as he is" (I John 3:2). In His present state Christ is "glorified," and if believers become like Him, they also shall be "glorified."

The moment of crisis at which this transformation will occur will be the return of Christ. At an indeterminate time in the course of human history, unknown except to the mind of God, He will reappear "to be glorified in his saints, and to be marvelled at in all them that believed" (II Thess. 1:10). His coming will be a logical parallel and a sequel to His own resurrection. Jesus left the earth visibly and bodily after the forty days of intermittent appearances to the disciples, and, with the possible exception of His appearances to Stephen (Acts 7:55, 56) and to Paul (I Cor. 15:8), he was never seen again by human eyes. His return will be correspondingly real, for the witnesses of the ascension predicted that "this Jesus [the risen Lord], who was received up from you into heaven, shall so come in like manner as ye beheld him going into heaven" (Acts 1:11).

Although the eschatological calendar cannot be plotted by specific dates, the succession of its main events is determined by the resurrection. "Christ the firstfruits; then they that are Christ's, at his coming. Then cometh the end, when he shall deliver up the kingdom to God" (I Cor. 15:23-24) gives the sequence. The new age which was introduced when Christ rose from the dead, asserting His transcendent authority over sin and death, will conclude with the resurrection of His church. The adverb "then," which occurs twice, is consequently chronological and marks definite intervals in the execution of the divine plan.

A distinction is drawn between the resurrection of the righteous and of the wicked, for the clause "then they that are Christ's, at his coming" (15:23) conveys the implication that those who are not Christ's will not be raised at the same moment. The resurrection of the wicked is separate from that of the righteous, yet subsequent to it and prior to the surrender of the perfected kingdom to the Father.

A more positive clue to the chronological sequence is provided by the book of Revelation, which asserts that the faithful who refused to renounce their faith and who consequently suffered martyrdom were raised at the beginning of Christ's reign, whereas "the rest of the dead did not come to life until the thousand years should be finished" (Rev. 20:5, original translation). The judgment of the remaining dead follows the kingdom and concludes Christ's judicial action.

The distinctive character of the resurrection of the righteous is supported by Paul's allusion in Philippians 3:11 to "the out-resurrection from among the dead" (a literal rendering of the Greek text: *tēn exanastasin ek tōn nekrōn*). The term which Paul used occurs only once and has been a puzzle to commentators. The unique nature of this expression, coupled with Paul's silence elsewhere concerning any special resurrection for believers, leaves some doubt whether he was speaking of a general hope or a particular reward. H. A. A. Kennedy says: "We are disposed to believe that Paul is thinking only of the resurrection of believers. . . . This is his usual standpoint. In the famous passage I Corinthians 15:12 ff. it is exclusively of Christians that he speaks. We have no information as to what he taught regarding a general resurrection. But considering that it is with spontaneous, artless letters we have to do, and not with theoretical discussions, it would be hazardous to say that he ignored or denied a general resurrection."[6]

---

[6] H. A. A. Kennedy, "Philippians" in *Expositor's Greek Testament* (New York: George H. Doran Company, n.d.), III, 457.

Paul did not deny a resurrection for all men; on the contrary, he had declared that all men must finally stand before the judgment seat of Christ to receive the reward of their deeds (II Cor. 5:10). The question is not *whether* they will be affected by the resurrection but *when,* and *in what order.* Whether this initial resurrection will include all believers in Christ or only a special group who are thus rewarded for outstanding service may be debatable. If Paul anticipated resurrection as a normal outcome of faith, he seemed unduly concerned about attaining it, but if he meant that it was bestowed as a prize for sacrifice or endurance, the meaning would be more easily understood.

A parallel in Hebrews illustrates the same principle: ". . . others were tortured, not accepting their deliverance; that they might obtain a better resurrection" (Heb. 11:35). The reference concerns the Maccabean martyrs, who chose to die rather than to transgress the law by partaking of unclean food. They esteemed the resurrection of the righteous better than that of compromisers and consequently refused to relinquish their convictions. The conclusion seems inevitable that the resurrection of the righteous will be different from that of the wicked.

The nature of the resurrection of the wicked is not described in detail. Scripture supplies hints which imply that it will be the negative counterpart of the resurrection of the righteous. For both believers and unbelievers some mode of existence will be created by which they will realize the full consequences of their deeds in the present life.

The two resurrections are mentioned in contrasting parallels. "And many of them that sleep in the dust of the earth shall awake, some to everlasting life, and some to shame and everlasting contempt" (Dan. 12:2). If the prospect of the believer is glory, the destiny of the unbeliever is gloom. The body with which he is clothed will suffer eternal defeat, frustration, and weakness. Because it bears forever the stamp of crooked character, the scars of conflicts, and the disfigurements of debauchery, it will be a painful reminder of his sins.

Jesus predicted that "the hour cometh, in which all that are in the tombs shall hear his voice, and shall come forth; they that have done good, unto the resurrection of life; and they that have done evil, unto the resurrection of judgment" (John 5:28-29). The pronouncement involves the added element of a retributive sentence pronounced upon the offender. Eternally fixed in a condition corresponding to their own sinful past, they will find their society both unendurable and inescapable. Their destiny may be the permanent crystallization of character in bodily form rather than the arbitrary infliction of an external penalty.

Paul spoke similarly of a resurrection "of the just and unjust" (Acts 24:15). As surely as there will be a resurrection for the one, there will be for the other. If salvation is brought to perfection by the endowment of a body which will express the highest experiences and aspirations, condemnation can be effected by a corresponding process. If the body of a righteous man will possess heightened beauty and efficiency, the body of a wicked man will comprise the sum of evil and depravity. If the righteous will be freed from debasing appetites, the wicked will be enslaved by them. The body could become a prison, confining its owner to the narrow and depressing consequences of his own sins, or it could be so keyed that its response to the character and presence of God would be painful. Hell need not be the gratuitous infliction of torture; it need only be the overpowering awareness of the existence of God to one who hated Him and whose every nerve would be set on edge by that consciousness.

R. McCheyne Edgar has suggested that the resurrection body of the wicked, being a gift of Christ, will serve as a check upon sin. "Will any reverential thinker imagine that a Risen Saviour will summon from the sepulchre the old bodies of the godless, filled with the sins of their youth? Is it not more consonant with all we know of Jesus, to believe that He will endow the wicked with bodies immortal, and exactly suited to the souls they are to enshrine?"[7]

To possess a body forever incapable of achieving the glories for which God made its owner, and to be reminded constantly of the sins of one's past might be a restraint against further wicked-

---

[7] R. McCheyne Edgar, *The Gospel of a Risen Saviour* (Edinburgh: T. & T. Clark, 1892), p. 330.

ness, but it would certainly be an unspeakable humiliation and shame.

Over the resurrection of the wicked Scripture mercifully draws a curtain of silence. One can only speculate by contrast with the destiny of the righteous what the fate of the unbelieving will be. The main thrust of revelation is concerned with salvation, not with damnation, for it was not God's prime choice that men should be condemned, but rather that they should enjoy Him and His provisions for them eternally. If they persistently reject His love, they can expect no other alternative than to continue existence apart from Him in a progressive alienation from His goodness and fellowship. The resurrection would be for them the point of fixation of their final doom, as it will be the ultimate reward for the righteous.

VIII   *The Pattern of Experience*

The annual recurrence of Easter, memorializing the empty tomb and the appearances of the Lord, and the Scripture read at a funeral service constitute for many Christians the limits of their knowledge of its significance. The unfortunate result of this constricted concept is a defective comprehension of the gospel. The resurrection cannot be relegated to the place of an auxiliary miracle corroborating apologetics, nor is it only the denouement of the unfolding plan of salvation. Because it marks the culmination of Christ's revelation and the supreme manifestation of God's power in a hostile world, it is also the essence and pattern of Christian experience.

The incarnate life of Christ is God's design for man's career. The Lord Jesus Christ participated in every normal activity, yet He did not succumb to the temptations that have induced the failure of the human race. His life was characterized by unblemished holiness, which the New Testament presents as a demonstration of divine power to be appropriated rather than as an example to be imitated. His precepts form the basis of spiritual and ethical standards, but the resurrection provides the dynamic by which they may be realized.

The pattern begins with the figure of death. Man apart from God is "dead through your trespasses and sins" (Eph. 2:1). Adam, by his initial act of disobedience, severed himself from God, the source of life, and consequently found himself alienated from his Creator, a stranger to His presence and a rebel against His will. When God said to Adam concerning the forbidden fruit, "in the day that thou eatest thereof thou shalt surely die" (Gen. 2:17), He did not mean that Adam would expire within twenty-four hours, for he long survived the expulsion from Eden. God meant rather that he would be cut off from the source of spiritual vitality. The account in Genesis reveals how shame, doubt, misunderstanding, and guilt intervened between man and his Creator. Adam died spiritually because the connection between him and the source of life was broken.

Time alone cannot heal this breach; on the contrary, persistence in sin can only widen it. Time fixes evil habits, ingrains base tendencies, and hardens the conscience against God. Self-reform is impossible, for an imperfect man cannot make himself perfect, nor undo the wrong that has already been done. One might as well speak of reforming a paralytic as of reforming a sinner, because he possesses no spiritual vitality. He is already under condemnation, awaiting the final execution of the sentence. Any amelioration of his condition must originate outside of himself.

Paradoxically, the predicament cannot be solved by man's internal struggles, since he does not possess the moral stamina to cope with evil. Neither can it be alleviated from without, since neither change of location nor ordinary external influence can mold the human will. Were a perfect man to enter the struggle with temptation and were a new life to penetrate spiritual death, victory might be attainable.

The incarnation and resurrection of Christ met both of these conditions. By taking upon Himself the nature of men, Christ entered into their state completely, except that He did not sin (Heb. 4:15). He became voluntarily subject to death that He might know its nature and power through immediate contact. If He were to take the sinner's place, He must share the totality of the sinner's experience.

The death of Christ is the epitome of sin's consequences, the total resultant of the encounter between uninhibited evil and absolute holiness. The shame of legal condemnation, the exposure to ridicule, the humiliation of public disgrace, and the intense physical suffering of the cross combined to inflict upon Jesus the worst that evil could accomplish. He endured every mental and physical agony that any man could bear, and calmly consigned His spirit to God in utter confidence. The manner of His death bespoke victory so convincingly that the pagan centurion said, "Truly this man was the Son of God" (Mark 15:39).

Even a victorious death is a negative triumph. Although Jesus died voluntarily (John 10:18) and confidently (Luke 23:46), the fact would still remain that He had not differed from all men unless He could defeat death itself. By accepting the sinner's place He proved Himself greater than sin, for He lived a life of holiness, and He did not succumb to the inevitable end of sin, for He rose from the dead. The resurrection thus became the proof of His conquest. It is the symbol of a new kind of life which reacts against the destructive effects of evil and overcomes them. The resurrection is, therefore, not only the historical confirmation of Christ's personal triumph but the demonstration of the essential power of Christian life.

The classic explanation of this principle is the sixth chapter of Paul's letter to the Romans. By using the death and resurrection of Christ as a norm, Paul created an objective standard which elevated spiritual experience above a purely subjective and experimental method of trial and error. After allowing for all possible differences of individual temperament and of environmental circumstances, there still remains a common rule by which the values of Christian living can be measured. Union with Christ in His death to sin and in His resurrection unto God is the keynote of a post-conversion career.

The first stage of this union is burial with Christ. "We were buried therefore with him through baptism into death" (Rom. 6:4). The rite of baptism denotes a burial. Whether the method used be sprinkling, affusion, or immersion, it is a token of being plunged under the waters of death, by which sin is condemned, punished, and renounced. The convert who accepts baptism confesses himself to be a sinner deserving the sentence which God has pronounced upon his sin, and the cross of Christ becomes for him the dividing line between former rebelliousness and present dedication. He avows that through the death of Christ the world has been crucified to him, and he to the world (Gal. 6:14). Turning from his sins, he relegates them to the grave.

The metaphor of burial does not imply impossibility of further sinning, but finality of decision. The disobedience and alienation of the past must be abandoned and forgotten. Although the memory of former transgressions may have a chastening and humbling effect, the sin itself must be forsaken lest its corruption vitiate the new life into which the believer enters.

Severance from sins avails little, however, unless some definite step be taken in the opposite direction. The Christian life is not merely a negation of evil but the positive assertion of a fresh moral and spiritual vitality. The second element of this symbolism is the new power which springs from union with Christ in resurrection, "that like as Christ was raised from the dead through the glory of the Father, so we also might walk in newness of life" (Rom. 6:4). Emerging from the waters of baptism completes the figure of rising to a new life, without which the Christian would remain spiritually inert. "Newness of life" implies an energy which enables man to accomplish what was previously impossible because of weakness.

Plutarch, an ancient Roman philosopher and writer, once attempted to make a corpse stand on its feet. Failing to achieve his purpose, he gave up the task in disgust with the comment, "Deest aliquid intus"—"Something is missing inside." A cleansed conscience needs more than an ideal to produce a life of holiness; there must be a new power within. The resurrection is the dynamic of Christian ethics. Christ, having risen from the dead, was freed completely from the power of death, for "death no more hath dominion over him" (Rom. 6:9). By union with Christ a Christian shares His liberty, not because he becomes instantly flawless, but because the power of Christ possesses and frees him.

A healthy body may harbor germs of many diseases, but they do not endanger it because its vitality is greater than the virulence of the bacteria. Only when the body is weakened by malnutrition or fatigue does illness threaten it. Similarly, Christ's implanted life can counteract the latent tendencies to evil that harass the Christian. The constant impartation of power stabilizes the will and provides resistance to the unremitting barrage of temptations from the outer world. Evil is not abolished, either without the Christian or within him, but the power of God is so applied that he need not succumb to the opposing pressure.

The resurrection sets the pattern for a new environment. Fish cannot live in air and oxen cannot live in water because neither has a constitution adapted to an alien element. A Christian who possesses the life of Christ can exist only in an atmosphere conducive to the support of that life. For this reason the Scripture says, "If then ye were raised together with Christ, seek the things that are above, where Christ is, seated on the right hand of God. Set your mind on the things that are above, not on the things that are upon the earth. For ye died, and your life is hid with Christ in God" (Col. 3:1-3). When Christ arose, His thoughts and purposes were fixed on the glory that He would share with the Father. In His last prayer with the disciples He petitioned the Father to glorify Him with the glory which they had together before the world was created (John 17:5). Later, when He appeared to Mary Magdalene He reminded her that He was about to ascend to the Father (20:17). He no longer felt at home on earth and desired to return speedily to the glory.

If a disciple follows his Lord, he also must reach upwards. Paul speaks of "the upward calling . . . in Christ Jesus" (Phil. 3:14), a phrase that is duplicated by the previously quoted passage from Colossians. An eagle that is born to soar in the open sky cannot be content in the confinement of a barnyard. His ambition and his strength are matched with the clouds and the mountain heights. Likewise a Christian who has partaken of the life of Christ should not be satisfied to grovel in sensuality or to live for ephemeral pleasures, however innocent they may seem.

The negative application of this pattern of death, burial, and resurrection is stated explicitly by Paul's word in Colossians. The first stage of death is prescribed for the "members which are upon the earth: fornication, uncleanness, passion, evil desire, and covetousness, which is idolatry" (Col. 3:5). The identification of the deeds with the members of the body implies that sin is not an accidental error but is ingrained into the functioning of personality. Vices are incongruous with Christian character and must be eliminated, for the Holy Spirit cannot operate effectively if such evils are voluntarily permitted to continue.

The negative work of death must be followed by the positive productiveness of resurrection life: "compassion, kindness, lowliness, meekness, long-suffering, forbearing one another . . . forgiving one another . . . and love." These virtues reflect the qualities which Christ exhibited on earth and are the beneficial effects which He imparts to the regenerate individual.

The model for Christians is not an abstract code of law or an impossible ideal of goodness, but Christ, who has proved His power to maintain a holy life under the most adverse conditions that a human being can endure. The attainment of this ideal depends upon the measure of control that He exercises upon the believer; the key is not imitation, it is regulation. Paul expressed this truth in his classic sentence, "it is no longer I that live, but Christ liveth in me: and that life which I now live in the flesh I live in faith, the faith which is in the son of God, who loved me, and gave himself up for me" (Gal. 2:20). Commitment to a Saviour whose power is available in present emergencies insures the development of Christian character.

The correspondence of the believer's experience to Christ's resurrection is susceptible of more extensive comparison. God "made us alive together with Christ . . . and raised us up with him, and made us to sit with him in the heavenly places, in Christ Jesus" (Eph. 2:5, 6). In these mystical words the language of Ephesians sets a new spiritual perspective. Life seems bewildering and aimless to those who are embroiled in its conflicts because they cannot visualize any single purpose in the multitude of confused events. By viewing the process from the divine standpoint, "the right hand of God," one can attain some comprehension of God's total design. His objective for the world is centered in Christ, through whom and for whom is was created

(Col. 1:16), and the process of its redemption and restoration has been epitomized in His personal conquest of destruction and decay. Sharing with Christ the seat "in the heavenlies" one can comprehend better his own place in God's total economy, for he realizes that his salvation comprises not only his own deliverance from sins and fears but also the creation of a new world of which he becomes a part.

This enlarged perspective is amply illustrated by the Epistle to the Ephesians, which stresses the unity of the church. Paul teaches that Jew and Gentile are drawn together into one body through Christ, who has become "our peace" (Eph. 2:14). God, having raised Him from the dead, "gave him to be head over all things to the church, which is his body, the fulness of him that filleth all in all" (1:22-23). United by their individual dependence on the one invisible Head, the members of the church of Christ are indissolubly joined together in devotion to His person and consecration to His will. Unitedly they share the spiritual resources of the Holy Spirit whom He has sent and the wisdom which He exercises in directing and governing them.

Being thus elevated with Him above the artificial boundaries of time, space, and race, they become part of a universal fellowship in which there is no room for provincialism. The individual Christian realizes that he participates in a great plan which God has been perfecting through the ages. Understanding this fact broadens his vision and intensifies his confidence that his work will not end in futility, however constricted and transitory it may seem.

Such a perspective promotes both faith and courage. The workman engaged in erecting a building can often see only the monotony and the petty annoyances of his task, the perspiration and dirt on his body, and the apparent interference from other workmen. The architect who holds the blueprints can see the coordination of the work, and can watch the progress as a whole. He knows the irritating hindrances that occur, and he waits patiently for them to correct themselves. Because the work is proceeding according to schedule, he has courage to believe that it will reach a satisfactory culmination. If the workman could

share the architect's knowledge, he would pursue his labor en-
thusiastically, knowing that it was part of a larger and more
enduring project.

The culmination of the present pattern will be the final resurrection of the body. The progress of spiritual growth is "from
glory to glory, even as from the Lord the Spirit" (II Cor. 3:18).
The Holy Spirit is the agent by whom the life of Christ is applied
to the believer, so that he grows into the likeness of the Saviour
and is gradually prepared to enter the "house not made with
hands, eternal, in the heavens" (5:1). The power which is now
realized inwardly and mystically will finally be manifested out-
wardly and physically when God's program is completed.

The perfection of this purpose is nowhere described in detail.
Numerous phrases, however, intimate its nature. Christ is the
prototype, for John says, "we shall be like him; for we shall see
him even as he is" (I John 3:2). "As he is" refers to His glorified
presence, and therefore believers will share the likeness of His
present state. By contemplating indirectly His glory "as in a
mirror" (II Cor. 3:18), they progress toward the day when the
gradual process will culminate in sudden realization. "This corruptible must put on incorruption, and this mortal must put on
immortality" (I Cor. 15:53). Freed from the oppressive hindrances of sin's environment and effects, they will enter into
"the liberty of the glory of the children of God" (Rom. 8:21).
Paul likens this crisis to "adoption," by which a child is publicly
acknowledged as a mature member of the family and is declared
to have attained his majority (Rom. 8:23). He will then be capable of enjoying the total heritage that God has prepared for
him and will realize fully his eternal destiny.

IX   *The Resurrection*
Today

The artless and straightforward narrative of the resurrection
of Christ in the Gospels presents a difficult dilemma for modern
thought. If, in order to avoid acceptance of a miracle which
would be embarrassing to the normative principles of science,
its genuineness be rejected, the whole structure of Christian truth
degenerates into a superstition containing at best an insecure
modicum of ethical principles. If, on the other hand, the fact
be freely admitted as an article of faith, the naturalistic interpretation of the world must be discarded. Can the Gospels be
taken as accurate historical reports, or are they idealized projections of theological teaching, stated in cultural terms which are
no longer relevant? Or do they embody a truth which cannot be
expressed adequately by the language of any culture, but which,
on the other hand, cannot be explained away by any intellectual
device?

The Biblical evidence for the verity and importance of the
resurrection is incontrovertible. Whether the Gospels be four
contemporaneous witnesses of equal value, or whether they represent successive stages of a tradition which increasingly magnifies
the miraculous element, they agree that Jesus rose from the dead
on the third day. The differences between them are no greater
than those between other firsthand sources of acknowledged

historic events, and from a purely literary standpoint they are worthy of equal credence.

In recent years, theological critics have become increasingly aware of the cogency of this evidence, and although they have been reluctant to concede the accuracy of all the statements of the Gospels, they have admitted the central truth. G. D. Yarnold, discussing the account of the empty tomb in Mark 16:1-8, says:

For was not the knowledge of the empty tomb the necessary first step to faith in the resurrection of the Lord? Entering, "they saw a young man sitting on the right side, clothed in a long white garment." Implicitly in this earliest narrative he is already an angel, although the word is not used; a messenger from God, sent to disclose a spiritual truth. In this first-century account the angel is manifest to sight and hearing. But to a modern intelligence their alleged visible appearance is a source of difficulty, and is naturally regarded as myth—no longer either useful, or necessary, for our own understanding of the truth of the gospel.[1]

Ramsey, in commenting on the same phenomenon in the Markan and Matthean accounts, holds that the stories were "embellished" with gratuitous additions, even prior to their being reduced to written form. Having reviewed Matthew's allusion to a great earthquake, the descent of an angel, and the paralysis of the guard, he adds, "Such is an editor's embroidery of his source; and if elaboration of the tradition took place in the written stage it is reasonable to think that it took place in the oral stage, too."[2]

The language of these current writers marks a mediating position between the skepticism of nineteenth-century rationalism, which dismissed the concept of physical resurrection as scientifically impossible, and the faith of historic Christianity, which has accepted the testimony of the Gospels at face value. Both Yarnold and Ramsey agree that an actual event took place which can become a foundation for faith; they admit that there must be a core of truth to be "embroidered." On the other hand, they

---

[1] G. D. Yarnold, *Risen Indeed* (New York: Oxford University Press, 1959), p. 17.

[2] A. Michael Ramsey, *The Resurrection of Christ* (Philadelphia: The Westminster Press, 1946), pp. 61, 62.

are uncertain just where a line should be drawn between sober fact and subjective fancy.

Obviously the problem is vexing for the average man who judges the world by his observation and who tends to accept a uniformitarian philosophy of its operation. For him miracles do not happen; in his opinion any unusual phenomenon is the effect of some natural law imperfectly understood or perhaps totally unformulated. He should remember that by his own premises "law" may be the action of God, whose customary method underlies "natural law," but whose freedom to do His personal will may occasionally be manifested in "miracle."

The accompaniments of the resurrection such as the angels, the clothing of Christ, the food that He ate in the presence of His disciples may pose questions difficult to answer. Why should there be disparity in the number of the angelic beings who appeared at the tomb? Why should a heavenly being need material clothing, or eat bread and fish? Are these concomitant features essentially absurd, accretions that must be stripped away in order that the pure truth of a "spiritual" resurrection may be preached without hindrance?

Whether the appearances of Jesus after the resurrection are to be accepted as objective contacts of the disciples with a material body or whether they were only projections of their memory of Him in the days before the Passion, these accompaniments would necessarily be normal. If Jesus had a tangible body, even though it were differently constituted from others, He would have to appear in clothing in order to avoid alarming the disciples. He partook of food, not because He needed nourishment, but in order to convince them that He was not an insubstantial wraith.

If His appearances were objective, it is not surprising that they should resemble the experiences of previous days, since a radical dissimilarity would be more bewildering than reassuring to the disciples. Reality depends upon a sense of continuity. If Jesus desired His followers to believe that He had risen from the dead, He would necessarily manifest Himself in a form that they would recognize, and would offer proof that His existence was independent of their imaginations. His being was not contingent upon material substance, but He chose to make it the vehicle of self-disclosure in order that those who witnessed the revelation might be fully assured of His reality.

Because of the uniquely convincing character and effects of these appearances, they cannot be dismissed abruptly as delusions. Recent writers who grapple with this problem tend to explain the visions as "objective" apparitions impressed upon the minds of the disciples by the Lord, who had already ascended. Such impressions would be "objective" because they were unsought and because they were imprinted on the consciousness of the recipients as vividly as any natural images perceived by the retina of the physical eye, but they would not emanate from a tangible body standing immediately before them.

Several varieties of this hypothesis have been proposed and rejected. The appearances cannot have been purely subjective illusions, conjured up by wishful thinking or daydreaming. Renan's dictum, "Heroes do not die,"[3] assumes that the disciples were stubbornly sure that Jesus would not die, and therefore, since they expected to see Him risen, they projected His image into the "appearances" recorded in the Gospels. According to the available evidence which is as reliable as the accounts of the appearances themselves, the disciples did not expect that Jesus would rise, and the entire experience of the resurrection was unanticipated and unsought. It could not have been superinduced by wishful thinking.

A second hypothesis equates the appearances of Jesus with spiritualistic séances, in which the personality of the dead Christ was reproduced through a medium or else manifested itself by ectoplasm. The varied circumstances of these appearances militates against such a theory. Jesus was manifested under conditions quite different from those of the ordinary séance. He appeared to the disciples at dawn on the shores of Galilee (John 21:4-14); to Mary Magdalene in the morning by the door of the empty tomb (20:11-17); to Cleopas and his companion on the

[3] E. Renan, *The Apostles,* translated from the original French (New York: Carleton, 1866), p. 55.

afternoon of the first day of the week (Luke 24:13-16); and to Paul at high noon on the Damascus road (I Cor. 15:8; Acts 26:13). In these instances no medium was present, nor did the procedures follow the usual method of conjuring up a spirit. Certainly the resurrection phenomena do not fall within the ordinary category of such apparitions.

As a compromise between abandoning completely the verity of the resurrection and accepting the full implications of the perpetuation of Jesus' physical body, Michael Clark has renewed the "telepathic" theory, though he has modified it in the direction of a fading materialism. According to his summary, the first appearances were definitely corporeal, though not material like our bodies; the later appearances were increasingly non-material.

Jesus died on the cross, but was raised from the dead by his Father. In his new state he was no longer clothed by the old material body of his incarnate life, but by some kind of spiritual body such as St. Paul attempts to describe for us.

Without a body of flesh, Jesus wished to convince his disciples that he was alive and had transcended death, and continue the teaching which Calvary had interrupted. He could not do this merely by impressing their minds with the certainty of his survival. Nobody else would have believed them, and they would not have had enough conviction to continue to believe in the face of opposition. . . .

Jesus therefore communicated with his disciples—we do not know how, so we call it "telepathy"—and caused their minds to project an apparition of his body as they had known it. This would demonstrate to them, in the only way in which they could understand, that it was really he who was teaching them and that he had truly conquered the powers of Death. . . .

The teaching which Jesus was giving his disciples and the doctrines which he was implanting in their minds, were projected by them along with the apparitional figure so that they heard the apparition giving them the teaching which Jesus wished them to absorb and reflect upon.[4]

---

[4] Michael Clark, *The Easter Enigma* (London: Faber and Faber, Ltd., 1959), pp. 194, 195.

Clark is obviously reluctant to surrender the objective reality of the resurrection, and adopts this hypothesis to evade the difficulties involved in the appearance and disappearance of a material body.

One may admit at the outset that "seeing" involves more than the physical effect of reflected light on the mechanism of the eye. The stimulus thus given must be relayed to the brain, and thence to the consciousness, which acts accordingly. Memory, which does not entail physical sight, can recall scenes and can be an equally potent stimulus. If it were possible for God to implant the reality of Christ's continuing existence and personal presence directly in the consciousness of the disciples without physical intervention, the resurrection would be no less real and no less a miracle. It would, furthermore, differ from a purely subjective illusion or from a psychic "manifestation."

The chief objection to this telepathic theory is the fact of the empty tomb. If Jesus manifested Himself solely by impressions transmitted by telepathy, while His body still reposed in Joseph's garden, the disciples might have been convinced that His personality had survived, but not that He had risen physically from the dead. On the other hand, if His body did disappear from the tomb, and they professed to have seen Him and to have eaten with Him, telepathy would be insufficient to account for the event.

To escape from this dilemma Clark asserts that a telepathic message from Christ affected the minds of the disciples, who then had a "mental projection" of the image of Jesus[5] and put into His mouth the words which accompanied the apparition. The disciples guessed that the apparition was the same body that Jesus had borne on the cross, but they were mistaken. The "body" which they saw would not have registered on a camera, nor would it have made sounds that could have been recorded on a tape.

In order to complete this hypothesis, the author is compelled to affirm that the concept of an actual material appearance is a mistake. "We disagree with the interpretation which Luke XXIV,

_____
[5] *Ibid.*, p. 211.

39 shows the disciples put on their experiences."[6] He even contends that "God deliberately caused the disciples to err by believing in a physical Resurrection because that would be less harmful than the otherwise inevitable mistake of thinking of Jesus as a disembodied ghost, one of the shades in Sheol."[7] His explanation assumes that the supposed error of the disciples was permitted in order that they might appeal more effectively to the thinking of their generation.

While it is true that revelation is progressive in character, God cannot stoop to deceit. To suggest that the appearances of Christ were "deliberately" presented as real when they were only telepathic communication demands more of the reader's credulity than the miracle would ask. If the fundamental statements of Scripture cannot be taken at face value in their original setting, one might as well relinquish any expectation of drawing sound conclusions from such elusive material.

Acceptance of the literary evidence does not predicate a complete knowledge of its nature. The physical composition of the resurrection body, the laws that govern its operation, and its relation to the visible world order remain in the realm of mystery. Nevertheless, the mystery cannot be dismissed by relegating it to irrationality or impossibility, for the deeper probing of natural phenomena discloses scientific problems of equal magnitude. The resurrection cannot be reproduced in a test tube or observed by a telescope. It can best be described as the intervention of divine power in the disintegrative process of decay, by which dissolution is arrested and the regenerative power of God is manifested.

The modern debate over the resurrection is not confined to opposing assessments of historical evidence. For many thinkers, the prime question is not whether the resurrection is real, but whether it is relevant. Reinhold Niebuhr, in a popular article, "The Religious Traditions of Our Nation," published in the *Saturday Evening Post,* said:

---

[6] *Ibid.,* p. 214.
[7] *Ibid.,* p. 215.

Incidentally, most modern Biblical scholars take it for granted that Christ's resurrection was not a public event in the same sense as the crucifixion, but rather a spiritual experience of his disciples, a symbol of the early Christian faith that Christ's death represented the climax of a historical drama in which both the divine mystery and the human situation were definitively clarified. The resurrection stories, however dubious as records of "public" historical events, are witnesses to the fact that the church, which was formed by the inspiration of the life and death of the man Jesus of Nazareth, did not regard his death as merely the martyrdom of a noble man but as a drama in which the ultimate mysteries about God and man were clarified.[8]

Dr. Niebuhr's estimate of the resurrection is typical of several modern theologians. He maintains that it may never have occurred in the same way that the crucifixion did—an event visible to all comers, incorporated in the public records of the Jewish and Roman officials, both attested by witnesses who observed the entire process and supported by natural probability. The process of the resurrection was not observed by anyone; only its results were visible. Since they seemed inherently incredible, it is easier to assume that the episode was a symbolic description of Jesus' victory over death, cast in this form by His followers to give greater coherence to the message which they preached. In fact, as long as the active revelation of God in the person of Christ is accepted, the miraculous return from the dead is inconsequential.

Karl Barth adopts a similar position in his commentary on Romans 6:4: ". . . the feature of the Resurrection . . . is a parable of our eternity. . . . We have already seen that the rising of Jesus from the dead is not an event in history elongated so as still to remain an event in the midst of other events. The Resurrection is the non-historical relating of the whole historical life of Jesus to its origin in God."[9]

---

[8] Reinhold Niebuhr, "The Religious Traditions of Our Nation," *Saturday Evening Post*, 233 (July 23, 1960), 26, 27, 45, 48.
[9] Karl Barth, *The Epistle to the Romans* (Oxford: University Press, 1933), p. 195.

Barth's recent testimony to the resurrection seems somewhat equivocal. Under his discussion of "Jesus, Lord of Time," he says:

We may relegate it [the Easter story] to the periphery, or regard it as an incidental and dispensable feature in the story. But whatever our own personal attitude to the resurrection may be (and there are many alternatives to choose from) we can at least agree on one point. . . . It is not peripheral to the New Testament, but central; not inessential or dispensable, but essential and indispensable. And it is all this, not in a different sense, but exactly in the sense in which the New Testament takes it. . . . Either we believe with the New Testament in the risen Jesus Christ, or we do not believe in him at all.[10]

Barth thus defends the centrality of the resurrection in Christian theology but does not at this point affirm a personal faith in the *bodily* resurrection.

Nevertheless, Barth seems to accept the verity of the physical accompaniments of the resurrection even though he does not consider them to be of prime importance. "Jesus Himself," he says, "did rise again and appear to His disciples. This is the content of the Easter history, the Easter time, the Christian faith, and Christian proclamation, both then and at all times."[11] Again, "It is impossible to erase the bodily character of the resurrection of Jesus and His existence as the Resurrected," he says. "Nor may we gloss over this element in the New Testament record of the forty days, as a false dualism between spirit and body has repeatedly tried to do. For unless Christ's resurrection was a resurrection of the body, we have no guarantee that it was the decisively acting Subject Jesus Himself, the *man* Jesus, who rose from the dead."[12]

Although the language quoted above intimates that Barth believes in the bodily resurrection of Christ, one cannot be quite sure what he means. Undoubtedly he adheres to the present exist-

---

[10] Karl Barth, *Church Dogmatics*, Vol. III, Part ii (Edinburgh: T. & T. Clark, [1960]), pp. 442, 443, 445.

[11] *Ibid.*, p. 445.

[12] *Ibid.*, p. 448.

ence of the person of Christ in a continuing state of conscious life. The emphasis on faith in the "Easter event" combined with a deprecation of the material accompaniments of the resurrection makes his reader wonder how far faith can extend without some foundation in experience.

Barth, however, is more conservative in his position than Bultmann; for where Barth is ambiguous, Bultmann is negative. The latter has introduced a more radical method of interpretation in "demythologization" (*Entmythologisierung*). He contends that the Bible was written by men steeped in the cultural concepts of their own day and writing to others who lived in and understood that culture. The teachings of Scripture, therefore, cannot be directly applied to the present generation, living in a different intellectual climate and consequently thinking in a different idiom. In the process of interpreting the Bible one must discard the forms of the past era and rephrase its teachings in a more acceptable modern style.

Within limits Bultmann's principle is workable, for it is obvious that figures of speech will change with culture. If the Bible were being written today it would probably contain allusions to automobiles, electronics, space flight, the United Nations, and numerous other things that were totally unknown two millenniums ago. On the other hand, occurrences affecting elemental human existence do not change radically. Birth, speech, work, and death remain the same, and no amount of philosophical verbiage will alter them.

Bultmann's view of the resurrection has been quite adequately represented by Burton H. Throckmorton in his recent work on *The New Testament and Mythology*. He offers three reasons why the resurrection cannot be accepted as a "proving miracle" for the meaning of the cross, and consequently of Jesus' life. "Moreover, the resurrection cannot be understood as a miracle that proves the meaning of the crucifixion even though it is so understood in the New Testament when it speaks of the empty tomb and of the bodily appearances. The resurrection cannot be a proving miracle because (a) it is unbelievable, (b) witnesses cannot prove it, and most important (c) because it is itself an object of faith and one object of faith cannot prove another."[13]

Bultmann's criticisms are not fatal to the miraculous nature of the resurrection, because he has failed to distinguish between an event that is improbable and one that is incredible. Admittedly Christ's resurrection is a unique phenomenon, for it differs even from the instances of resuscitation accomplished by the prophets and by Jesus Himself. If it were not unique, it would not be significant. Whether or not one can believe that such an event actually occurred will be determined by his presuppositions rather than by the historical record. The written accounts are as valid as any history can be; the problem lies in their interpretation. Granted an omnipotent personal God who seeks to reveal Himself through the application of His power to the salvation of men, the resurrection is not unbelievable. On the contrary, it is the logical result of the conflict between the powers of good and of evil, between God and death. Death was decreed by God to be the check and punishment of sin (Gen. 3:3; Rom. 6:23), but He never intended that it should defeat His purpose. God, to be God, must win the ultimate victory in the same field where the original failure occurred. If the first Adam succumbed to death, the second Adam must triumph in life. The negation of resurrection would be less believable than the event which the New Testament relates.

The objection that "witnesses cannot prove it" is based on an artificial antithesis of knowledge and faith. Throckmorton argues:

If Jesus had been raised in a physical body, his resurrection would have been a historical event to be demonstrated simply by pointing to him; and Jesus would have been seen by multitudes in Galilee and Jerusalem, and presumably on the road in between by men and women who had never been his disciples. All would have believed, for his resurrection would have been revealed to all. No; his resurrection would have been *revealed* to no one, for it would have been a historical event. If Jesus' resurrection had been a historical event, none could have *be-*

[13] Burton H. Throckmorton, *The New Testament and Mythology* (Philadelphia: The Westminster Press, [1959]), p. 57.

lieved, for it would have been *revealed* to none, and would have been *known* by all. It would have been an event to be recorded as verifiable history, rather than an event to be preached as revelation: but it was the latter. It was the event in which God revealed, to eyes that could see, the significance of the crucifixion and the ultimate meaning of life. What I can see and hear and touch, I know, I do not believe; but I desire to believe more than to know.[14]

He assumes that any fact substantiated by witnesses cannot possibly become an object of faith. If, therefore, the resurrection is a cardinal article of faith to those who received the revelation, it is not a part of provable history, and witnesses are consequently irrelevant.

The New Testament, however, does join knowledge and faith. The disciples of Jesus were essentially witnesses, for they declared what they had seen and heard (I John 1:1-3). Between the historical occurrences of the Easter week and the continuing awareness of the presence of Christ no barrier existed. The material manifestations in space and time afforded the foundation for the faith that extended beyond the tangible and temporal facts. John, standing within the empty tomb and gazing at the graveclothes, "saw, and believed" (John 20:8). The facts which he observed compelled him to acknowledge the spiritual reality that transcended them.

One may object that the written accounts were composed much later than the beginning of public preaching and therefore represent a modification or exaggeration of the original testimony, so that the "history" is only a fabricated illustration of the concept of resurrection. Such a conclusion is unacceptable because it implies an unreliability of the records that would jeopardize not only the history but also faith itself. If the knowledge of the witnesses is irrelevant, their faith becomes illusory.

Furthermore, the effectiveness of a witness depends upon his reliability and upon the attitude of the person to whom his testimony is given. If witnesses could not prove the resurrection, it was not because they lacked data but because the recipients

---

[14] *Ibid.,* p. 70.

of their message were impervious to truth. No proof is convincing to a person who has closed his mind. If he thinks that testimony is unbelievable, it will fail to carry conviction, regardless of the strength of supporting evidence.

The third criticism, that one object of faith cannot prove another, is subtle but not decisive. Any historical event may become an object of faith once it has occurred. Since it can never be exactly repeated, knowledge must depend on records and upon consequences, for witnesses will not survive many years. Historians believe that Columbus discovered America in 1492, but it would be impossible to re-enact the episode with the same personnel, equipment, and surroundings in order to demonstrate its verity. The earliest written accounts provide the basis of confidence; faith in the reality follows. The discovery of America thus accepted becomes in turn another link in historical thinking concerning the development of American civilization. Similarly, the records of the resurrection supply the "proof" upon which a larger faith builds the concept of eternal life in Christ.

If Bultmann's criticisms be carried to their logical conclusion, the objective historical character of the resurrection must be abandoned. To quote Throckmorton, "The descriptions of the resurrection that are recorded in the New Testament are, then, to be read and understood as mythological. They are not to be taken literally as though they were self-authenticating accounts of a provable occurrence."[15] The language of historical revelation is thus reduced to ambiguous symbols which have no stable meaning, but which must be revaluated for every generation. "Demythologization" implies that the physical reality of an empty grave or the disposition of the graveclothes would be only the convenient method of expressing in the language of the first century that Jesus had survived death. The literal meaning of these statements would be inconsequential, and only the general truths imbedded in them would remain cogent.

Such a view does injustice to the writers of the New Testament. Writing for a generation later than the time of Jesus, and for a people who lived outside of Palestine, they might have

---

[15] *Ibid.*, p. 78.

utilized a symbolism drawn from their immediate surroundings, as Plato did in some of his *Dialogues*. On the contrary, they stressed the physical phenomena accompanying the resurrection because they believed that the historical facts had permanent validity. Although they were puzzled by these events, they did not regard the evidence as mythological, nor did they attempt to explain it. Had the witnesses created the stories for illustrative purposes, they would not have mentioned their own bewilderment. They recorded their experience in simple and direct words insofar as it was germane to the proclamation of their message, and left the unexplained aspect for the review of others.

To assert that they deliberately represented the "event" of the resurrection as an outward physical occurrence for the sake of making it comprehensible to a materially minded public implies either that they falsified the facts or that their reasoning was far more subtle than their writings imply. The Gospels bear no trace of double meaning. To impose allegorical significance upon them contradicts the plain understanding of history. Although one may concede that belief in the person of Christ rather than in the activities connected with Him constitutes saving faith, it is still true that the nature of the person can be known only through these activities. To dissolve the facts into meaningless myth is no real aid to faith.

Richard Niebuhr defines Bultmann's concept of *myth* as "the typical expression of that naïve mentality that projects internally apprehended meanings upon the screen of the cosmos, quite heedless of the difference between objective and subjective truth."[16] He implies that there is an intrinsic confusion between external fact and inward consciousness in the minds of the writers of the New Testament. They were confident that Jesus was alive, and thus expressed their assurance by predicating the material manifestations. Such a conclusion does injustice to these men. They stressed the physical phenomena accompanying the resurrection because they believed that their faith was permanently valid. Although the resurrection becomes a pattern of inner

---

[16] Richard R. Niebuhr, *Resurrection and Historical Reason* (New York: Charles Scribner's Sons, 1957), p. 54.

spiritual life, the factual event must initiate the pattern. Every copy presupposes an original, and if the Christian life is a continuous resurrection, it is based on the one great historic act by which God demonstrated His power over death and assured believers of a similar victory.

One further comment on Bultmann's method might be suggested. If the language of the New Testament means only that the truth of resurrection was expressed as a phenomenon to make it intelligible for the mentality of the first century, what guarantee does Bultmann offer that his explanation is more valid? Has he "demythologized" the narrative of the Bible only to "remythologize" it for the twentieth century? Is his personal interpretation more worthy of permanent credence than the original assertion that Jesus rose bodily from the grave? If it be granted that the resurrection narratives are "myth" in the technical sense of that term, Bultmann has failed to explain adequately why the myth should take the particular form that it did, or why the thought-forms of the present should necessitate a complete abandonment of the language of the past. If "myth" means essentially the definition of a concept in terms derived from the usages of a prevailing culture, the statements of the New Testament are as valid today as ours will be a millennium hence.

"Myth," then, is a convenient method of conveying truth in a popular figure which becomes a technical term. If the terms become increasingly unfamiliar to succeeding generations, either their meanings must be kept alive by arbitrary definition or else the concepts must be expressed in newer and more familiar images. Such redefinition, however, does not alter their essential value, nor does it mean that they are no longer relevant. Rather, it sets the established truths in a new light, preserving their variety and intensifying their relevancy.

Quite possibly the future may bring some new explanation of the resurrection, but the fact will remain that Jesus returned from the dead to resume physical existence and to renew contact with His disciples. Such is the plain statement of the Gospel witnesses which no amount of sophistry can discredit.

Can these facts be relevant to modern life? Will they fit the intellectual mood of this scientific era? To be sure, they cannot be re-enacted as an experiment in chemistry can be repeated at will in the laboratory. They are not reactions of matter subject to the will of an investigator but are events in the life of a person which can never be repeated with identical movement and emotion. The birth of a child cannot occur more than once, yet the birth itself is a permanent reality which cannot be undone or disputed.

In similar fashion the resurrection of Christ remains the great unshakable reality of the ages. He can never die and rise again; He has died to sin once for all, and He lives now unto God. There can be no change in the imagery, for life and death are basic to all existence and cannot be defined in more comprehensive terms. Because they are ultimate, they are comprehensible in every generation and are always vital to every sphere of human relationship.

Bibliography

The Ante-Nicene Fathers. Edited by Alexander Roberts and James Donaldson. American Reprint of Edinburgh Edition. 10 vols. Grand Rapids, Mich.: Wm. B. Eerdmans Publishing Company, 1951.

The Apocryphal New Testament, being the Apocryphal Gospels, Acts, Epistles, and Apocalypses with other narratives and fragments. Translated by Montague Rhodes James. Oxford: The Clarendon Press, 1955.

The Apostolic Fathers. Translated by Kirsopp Lake. 2 vols. London: William Heinemann; New York: G. P. Putnam's Sons, 1919.

Barth, Karl. *Die Auferstehung der Toten, eine akademische Vorlesung über I Kor. 15.* München: Chr. Kaiser, 1924.

————. *Church Dogmatics.* Vol. III, *The Doctrine of Creation,* part ii. Translated by Harold Knight, G. W. Bromiley, J. K. S. Reid, R. H. Fuller. Edinburgh: T. & T. Clark, [1960].

————. *Dogmatics in Outline.* Translated by G. T. Thomson. New York: Philosophical Library, [1947]; Harper Torchbooks, 1959.

————. *The Epistle to the Romans.* Translated from the Sixth Edition by Edwyn C. Hoskyns. Oxford: University Press; London: Humphrey Milford, 1933.

Bornhaeuser, Karl. *The Death and Resurrection of Jesus Christ.* Translated by Rev. A. Rumpus. London: Independent Press, 1958.

Branton, Rodney. "The Resurrection in the Early Church," in *Early Christian Origins,* edited by Allen Wikgren. Chicago: Quadrangle Books, 1961.

Bruce, F. F. *Commentary on the Book of Acts,* in *New International Commentary on the New Testament.* Grand Rapids, Mich.: Wm. B. Eerdmans Publishing Company, 1954.

Budge, E. A. Wallis. *Egyptian Ideas of the Future Life.* London: Kegan Paul, Trench, Trubner, & Company, Ltd., 1900.

———. *Osiris and the Egyptian Resurrection.* 2 vols. London: P. L. Warner, 1911.

Bultmann, Rudolf. *History and Eschatology.* The Gifford Lectures, 1955. Edinburgh: University Press, 1957; New York: Harper Torchbooks, 1962.

———. *Jesus Christ and Mythology.* New York: Charles Scribner's Sons, [1958].

Cadbury, Henry J. "Acts and Eschatology," in *The Background of the New Testament and Its Eschatology,* edited by W. D. Davies and D. Daube. *Studies in Honour of Charles Harold Dodd.* Cambridge: University Press, 1956.

Canfield, F. W. "Man in His Time," *Scottish Journal of Theology,* III (June, 1950), 127-148.

Carlston, Charles Edward. "Transfiguration and Resurrection," *Journal of Biblical Literature,* LXXX (1961), 233-240.

Charles, R. H. *A Critical History of the Doctrine of the Future Life in Israel, in Judaism, and in Christianity.* (Jowett Lectures for 1898-99. London: Adam & Charles Black, 1899.

Clarke, W. K. Lowther. *New Testament Problems.* New York: The Macmillan Company, 1929. See pp. 102-107: "What Became of Our Lord's Body?"

Creed, J. M. "The Conclusion of the Gospel According to St. Mark," *Journal of Theological Studies,* XXXI (January, 1930), 175-182.

Cullmann, Oscar. *Immortality of the Soul or Resurrection of the Dead?* The Ingersoll Lectures. Harvard University, 1954-55. London: The Epworth Press, 1958.

Donehoo, James D. *The Apocryphal and Legendary Life of Christ.* New York: The Macmillan Company, 1903. See especially Chapter XXV, "The Resurrection," pp. 396-409.

Durrwell, Francis X. *The Resurrection: A Biblical Study.* Translated by Rosemary Sheed. Introduction by Charles Davis. New York: Sheed & Ward, 1960.

Edgar, R. McCheyne. *The Gospel of a Risen Saviour.* Edinburgh: T. & T. Clark, 1892.

Enslin, Morton S. "And That He Hath Been Raised," *Jewish Quarterly Review,* XLIII (1952-53), 27-56.

Forell, George W. *The Protestant Faith.* Englewood Cliffs, N.J.: Prentice-Hall, Inc., 1960.

Fuller, Reginald H. "The Resurrection of Jesus Christ," *Biblical Research*, IV (1960), 8-24.

Geldenhuys, Norval. *Commentary on Luke*, in *New International Commentary on the New Testament*. Grand Rapids, Mich.: Wm. B. Eerdmans Publishing Company, 1956.

Gilmour, S. McLean. "The Christophany to More Than Five Hundred Brethren," *Journal of Biblical Literature*, LXXX (1961), 248-252.

Goguel, Maurice. *The Birth of Christianity*. Translated from the French by H. C. Snape. New York: The Macmillan Company, 1954.

Gordon, Ernest. *Life of A. J. Gordon*. New York: Fleming H. Revell Company, 1896.

Grant, F. C. *An Introduction to New Testament Thought*. Nashville: Abingdon Press, 1950.

Grant, R. M. "Ignatius of Antioch," *Twentieth Century Encyclopedia of Religious Knowledge*, edited by Lefferts A. Loetscher. 2 vols. Grand Rapids, Mich.: Baker Book House, 1935, Vol. I.

Kennedy, H. A. A. "Philippians," *Expositor's Greek Testament*, edited by W. Robertson Nicoll. New York: George H. Doran Company, n.d. Vol. III, pp. 397-473.

Knox, John. *The Death of Christ: The Cross of New Testament History and Faith*. Nashville: Abingdon-Cokesbury Press, 1958.

Knox, W. L. "The Ending of Mark's Gospel," *Harvard Theological Review*, XXXV (January, 1942), 13-23.

Kohler, Kaufman. "Resurrection," *Jewish Encyclopedia*, X, 382a-385a.

Lake, Kirsopp. *The Historical Evidence for the Resurrection of Jesus Christ*. New York: G. P. Putnam's Sons, 1907.

Latham, Henry. *The Risen Master*. Cambridge: Deighton Bell & Company, 1901.

Legge, F. *The Worship of Osiris and Its Dramatization*, in *Forerunners and Rivals of Christianity*. Vol. I. Cambridge: University Press, 1915.

Martin-Achard, Robert. *From Death to Life*. Translated by John P. Smith. Edinburgh: Oliver and Boyd, 1960.

Mascall, E. L. *Christian Theology and Natural Science*. Bampton Lectures, 1956. New York: The Ronald Press Company, 1956.

Moore, George Foot. *Judaism in the First Centuries of the Christian Era*. 3 vols. Cambridge: Harvard University Press, 1932.

Morris, A. E. "The Narratives of the Resurrection of Jesus Christ," *The Hibbert Journal*, XXXIX (April, 1941), 309-324.

Niebuhr, Reinhold. "The Religious Traditions of Our Nation," *Saturday Evening Post*, 233 (July 23, 1960), 26, 27, 45, 48.

Niebuhr, Richard R. "The Problem of Preaching at Easter,"
    Christian Century, LXXVII (April 6, 1960), 410-412.
————. *Resurrection and Historical Reason*. New York: Charles
    Scribner's Sons, 1957.
Nock, Arthur D. "Appended Note on the Resurrection," in
    Essays on the Trinity, edited by A. E. J. Rawlinson. New York:
    Longmans, Green and Company, 1928.
Perry, Michael C. *The Easter Enigma*. London: Faber and Faber,
    Ltd., 1959.
Prat, Fernand. *The Theology of St. Paul*. English translation of
    11th French Edition. Westminster, Md.: The Newman Book-
    shop, 1950.
Ramsey, A. Michael. *The Resurrection of Christ*. Philadelphia:
    The Westminster Press, 1946.
Renan, Ernest. *The Apostles*. Translated from the original
    French. New York: Carleton, 1866.
Robertson, Archibald, and Alfred Plummer. *A Critical and Exe-
    getical Commentary on the First Epistle of Paul to the
    Corinthians*. New York: Charles Scribner's Sons, 1911.
Robinson, J. A. "The Resurrection Appearances," *Journal of
    Theological Studies*, XIV (January, 1913), 196-206.
Robinson, James M. *A New Quest of the Historical Jesus*. Naper-
    ville, Ill.: Alec R. Allenson, Inc., [1959].
Robinson, William Childs. *Christ, the Hope of Glory*. Grand
    Rapids, Mich.: Wm. B. Eerdmans Publishing Company, 1945.
Schürer, Emil. *A History of the Jewish People in the Time of
    Christ*. Second Revised Edition. Translated by Sophia Taylor
    and Rev. Peter Christie. Division II, Vols. II & III. New York:
    Charles Scribner's Sons, 1891.
Schweitzer, Albert. *The Quest of the Historical Jesus*. Second
    English Edition. London: Adam & Charles Black, 1936.
Scott, Ernest F. "The History of the Early Church: The Begin-
    nings," in *Interpreter's Bible*, Vol. VII. New York: Abingdon-
    Cokesbury Press, 1951.
Smedes, Lewis. "Does Karl Barth Believe in the Resurrection of
    Jesus Christ?" *Reformed Journal*, XII (April, 1962), 10-13.
Smith, David. *In the Days of His Flesh*. Eighth Edition. New
    York and London: Hodder & Stoughton, n.d.
Smith, Wilbur M. "The Third Day According to the Scriptures,"
    Sunday School Times, March 24, 1928, pp. 187, 188.
————. "The Deeper Meanings of 'Three' in the Scriptures,"
    Sunday School Times, March 31, 1928, pp. 207, 208.
————. "Resurrection and the Pagan Religions," *Sunday School
    Times*, April 7, 1928, pp. 220, 221.

————. "The Third Day According to the Scriptures," *Sunday School Times*, July 14, 1928, p. 418.

————. *The Supernaturalness of Christ*. Boston: W. A. Wilde Company, 1940. See Chapter VI, "The Historical Reality of Christ's Resurrection," pp. 189-231.

————. *Therefore Stand*. Boston: W. A. Wilde Company, 1945. See Chapter VIII, "The Resurrection from the Dead," pp. 359-437.

Sparrow-Simpson, W. J. *Our Lord's Resurrection*. London: Longmans, Green and Company, Ltd., 1905.

————. *The Resurrection and Modern Thought*. New York: Longmans, Green and Company, Ltd., 1911.

Spicq, C. *L'Épitre aux Hébreux*. Troisième Édition. 2 vols. Paris: Librairie Lecoffre, J. Gabalda et Cie., 1952.

Stauffer, Ethelbert. *Jesus and His Story*. Translated from the German by Richard and Clara Winston. New York: Alfred A. Knopf, Inc., 1960.

Swete, H. B. "The Resurrection of the Flesh," *Journal of Theological Studies, XVIII* (January and April, 1917), 135-141.

Tertullianus, Quintus Septimus Florens. *Concerning the Resurrection of the Flesh*. Translated by A. Souter. (*Translations of Christian Literature*, Series 2, Latin Texts.) London: S.P.C.K., 1922.

Thornton, L. S. *The Common Life in the Body of Christ*. London: Dacre Press, n.d.

Throckmorton, Burton H., Jr. *The New Testament and Mythology*. Philadelphia: The Westminster Press, [1959].

Vos, Geerhardus. "The Pauline Doctrine of the Resurrection," *Princeton Theological Review*, XXVII (January, 1929), 1-35.

Wolfson, Harry A. "Immortality of the Soul and the Resurrection in the Church Fathers." Ingersoll Lecture. *Harvard Divinity School Bulletin*, 1956-57. Cambridge: Harvard University, 1957.

Wright, G. E., and Reginald H. Fuller. *The Book of the Acts of God*. Garden City, N.Y.: Doubleday and Company, 1960.

Yarnold, G. D. *Risen Indeed*. New York: Oxford University Press, 1959.

Index of Names and Subjects

Index of Names and Subjects

Index of Scripture References

Index of Scripture References

OLD TESTAMENT

NEW TESTAMENT

APOCRYPHA AND PSEUDEPIGRAPHA

Format by Mort Perry
Set in Linotype Baskerville
Composed, printed and bound by The Haddon Craftsmen, Inc.
HARPER & ROW, PUBLISHERS, INCORPORATED